Kelly Ruth Winter

MARILYNNE ROBINSON is the author of the novels
Housekeeping; Gilead, winner of the Pulitzer Prize; and
Home, and of three books of nonfiction, *Mother Country, The Death of Adam,* and *Absence of Mind.* She teaches
at the University of Iowa Writers' Workshop.

ALSO BY MARILYNNE ROBINSON

FICTION

Housekeeping

Gilead

Home

NONFICTION

Mother Country: Britain, the Welfare State and Nuclear Pollution

The Death of Adam: Essays on Modern Thought

*Absence of Mind: The Dispelling of Inwardness from the Modern
Myth of the Self*

Additional Praise for *When I Was a Child I Read Books*

"Robinson's great virtue as an essayist is her ability to combine a deep knowledge of this country's literary, intellectual, and religious canon with a demotic, impassioned tone that is American in the highest sense.... For those who prefer their liberal American dream in the language of Ralph Waldo Emerson, Walt Whitman, and Emily Dickinson, Robinson has, for the past three decades, been the standard-bearer."   —*Bookforum*

"Robinson is an American original.... [Her voice] reveals a soul that burns with a hard gem-like flame and needs to be added to our national dialogue."   —Allen Barra, *The Atlantic*

"It matters little what Robinson is writing about or where she's going.... Her thinking is so bright with clarity, her phrasings so handsomely sweetened, that tailing her upriver is one of the great pleasures in life."   —*The Daily Beast*

"Robinson is best known for her fiction, but at her best she's a wise, droll, and incisive essayist.... [These pieces] are enlightening and a pleasure to read.... Superb." —*The Kansas City Star*

"It is difficult not to quote Ms. Robinson at length, so finely calibrated are her sentences.... This book is a tool for those who would be archaeologists of their own thinking."
—*The New York Observer*

"Having read these essays, I have a better understanding of the sort of mind that could create *Gilead,* a novel of quiet grace, and *Housekeeping,* a book so beautiful and otherworldly that at times it threatens to float away altogether."
—Maggie Galehouse, *The Houston Chronicle*

"When I say that I love Marilynne Robinson's work, I'm not talking about half of it; I'm talking about every word of it. . . . I have read and loved a lot of literature about religion and religious experience—Tolstoy, Dostoevsky, Flannery O'Connor, the Bible—but it's only with Robinson that I have actually felt what it must be like to live with a sense of the divine."

—Mark O'Connell, *NewYorker.com*

"The pieces in *Child* capture attention and stick with the reader long after the book is done. . . . It does not get any better than this."   —*Richmond Times-Dispatch*

When I Was a Child
I Read Books

·

MARILYNNE
ROBINSON

PICADOR

———

Farrar, Straus and Giroux

New York

www.picadorusa.com
www.twitter.com/picadorusa • www.facebook.com/picadorusa
picadorbookroom.tumblr.com

Picador® is a U.S. registered trademark and is used by Farrar, Straus and
Giroux under license from Pan Books Limited.

For book club information, please visit www.facebook.com/picadorbookclub
or e-mail marketing@picadorusa.com.

Some of these essays originally appeared, in slightly different form, in the
following publications: *Brick Magazine* ("When I Was a Child"); *Christianity
and Literature* ("Wondrous Love"); *The Chronicle of Higher Education* ("Freedom
of Thought," originally titled "Freedom to Think"); *Commonweal*
("Imagination and Community"); *The Nation* ("Austerity as Ideology");
and *Salmagundi* ("The Fate of Ideas: Moses").

Designed by Jonathan D. Lippincott

The Library of Congress has cataloged the Farrar, Straus and Giroux edition
as follows:

Robinson, Marilynne.
      When I was a child I read books / Marilynne Robinson.—1st ed.
      p.   cm.
      ISBN 978-0-374-29878-4
      I. Title.
   PS3568.O3125W47 2012
   814'.54—dc23

                                                                2011041206

Picador ISBN 978-1-250-02405-3

First published in the United States by Farrar, Straus and Giroux

First Picador Edition: February 2013

10 9 8 7 6 5 4 3

For my brother David Summers,
first and best of my teachers

Contents

Preface

Writing in 1870, Walt Whitman said, "America, if eligible at all to downfall and ruin, is eligible within herself, not without; for I see clearly that the combined foreign world could not beat her down. But these savage, wolfish parties alarm me. Owning no law but their own will, more and more combative, less and less tolerant of the idea of ensemble and of equal brotherhood, the perfect equality of the States, the ever-overarching American Ideas, it behooves you to convey yourself implicitly to no party, nor submit blindly to their dictators, but steadily hold yourself judge and master over all of them." And he said, "It is the fashion of dillettants [*sic*] and fops (perhaps I myself am not guiltless,) to decry the whole formulation of the active politics of America, as beyond redemption, and to be carefully kept away from. See that you do not fall into this error. America, it may be, is doing very well upon the whole, notwithstanding these antics of the parties and their leaders, these half-brained nominees, the many ignorant ballots, and many elected failures and blatherers." These passages come from Whitman's long essay *Democratic Vistas*, a virtual hymn of praise to America, and to Democracy, words which for him are interchangeable.

It is true that the period after the Civil War was a low point in American political history. And it is true also that the country came through it all at last, fairly intact by the standards that apply in such cases. This is reassuring to consider, since we now live in a political environment characterized by wolfishness and filled with blather. We have the passive pious, who feel they have proved their moral refinement in declaring the whole enterprise bankrupt, and we have the active pious, who agree with them, with the difference that they see some hope in a hastily arranged liquidation of cultural assets.

It was Whitman's faith that a great presiding spirit of Democracy would check, or correct for, the worst deficiencies of the civilization. It may indeed have been that ideal that kept us on course, or allowed us finally to find our way back to a better and healthier national life, then and in all the other periods in our history when our politics have seemed to be beyond redemption. Whitman says Democracy "is a great word, whose history, I suppose, remains unwritten, because that history has yet to be enacted." It is for him like the word "Nature" in that its history, therefore its definition, remains partial and tentative, though some valuable phrases and paragraphs have been added from time to time.

What if we have ceased to aspire to Democracy, or even democracy? What if the words "Democracy" and "America" are severed, and no longer imply each other? It is not unusual now to hear that we have lost our values, that we have lost our way. In the desperations of the moment, justified or not, certain among us have turned on our heritage, the country that has emerged out of generations of attention to public education, public health, public safety, access to suffrage, equality under law. It turns out, by their reckoning, that the country they call the greatest on earth has spent most of its history acting against its own (great) nature, and that the enhancements of life it has provided for the generality of its people, or to phrase it more democratically, that the people have provided for themselves, have made its citizens weak and dependent. How the greatest nation on earth maintains this exalted status while burdened with a population these patriots do not like or respect is an interesting question, certainly. In any case, the return to traditional values seems to them to mean, together with a bracing and punitive severity toward the vulnerable among us, the establishment of a kind of religious monoculture we have never had and our institutions have never encouraged.

Law in seventeenth-century Maryland forbade the use of the words "papist" (Catholic) or "round-head" (Puritan), fighting words in the Old World whose effects were muted here by methods still familiar to us. We learned early to live with diversity, at least by the standards of the time. It is useful to remember that the terrible Thirty Years War (1618–1648) was fought among European Christians during the early period of European settlement in America, and that New England was largely populated by British Protestant refugees of religious oppression and warfare in Protestant Britain. What might look like homogeneity in nostalgic retrospect was felt and acted upon as intolerable difference justifying enormity in these cultures of origin. Our national ancestors generally managed, by the standards then prevailing, to avoid encouraging the same conflicts here. Now it is seen as un-American in certain quarters to reject participation in the bitter excitements that can surround religious difference. This is a crucially important instance of self-declared patriots attacking the very substance of our heritage.

We have seen bad times and we will see more of them, like any other human community. The question is always whether America is indeed doing well upon the whole, whether the civilization at any present time is strong and resilient enough to sustain itself despite the crisis of the moment, or the decade, or the generation, and despite the bent toward malice and nonsense that is always present anywhere but seems harder to resist during periods of crisis.

What has been the basis of the enduring health that has so far made for the stability and the dynamism of the country? It is always necessary to stipulate, though of course it should be assumed, that a statement like this one implies comparison with the human norm, not with Utopia. As societies go, we have enjoyed the kind of prosperity and advancement that is possible only where there is domestic peace. We have managed this at the same time that we have created a population whose origins are increasingly various. The canard that associates "heterogeneity" with conflict and instability would have to be reexamined if comparison were made between America and countries that claim to be homogeneous or insist that they must be. The modern history of Europe is highly relevant here.

We are blessed with the impossibility of arriving at a definition of America that is either exhaustive or final not only because of our continuously changing and self-transforming population but also, as Whitman says, because we have never fully achieved democracy. This is a very reasonable light in which to consider a mingled heritage, full of lapses and errors and therefore often said to be hypocritical or failed, even by those who see themselves as its defenders. By Whitman's lights this process of discovery, with all its setbacks, is a splendid, metaphysically brilliant passage in human history. It is moved by the power of religious imperative because it honors and liberates the sacred human person. He says:

> There is, in sanest hours, a consciousness, a thought that rises, independent, lifted out from all else, calm, like the stars, shining eternal. This is the thought of identity—yours for you, whoever you are, as mine for me. Miracle of miracles, beyond statement, most spiritual and vaguest of earth's dreams, yet hardest basic

fact, and only entrance to all facts. In such devout hours, in the midst of the significant wonders of heaven and earth, (significant only because of the Me in the centre,) creeds, conventions fall away and become of no account before this simple idea. Under the luminousness of real vision, it alone takes possession, takes value.

Language like this makes clear how far our vocabulary has drifted over the generations. So far from the sense of radical uniqueness Whitman evokes here, identity seems now to imply membership in a group, through ethnicity or affinity or religion or otherwise. Rather than acknowledging the miraculous privilege of existence as a conscious being (and, considering the overwhelming odds against anyone's existence, the word "miraculous" is an appropriate superlative), it has reference now to knowing one's place, culturally and historically speaking. And this is taken to be a good thing. Whitman himself has been charged with rampant egoism for pondering and celebrating the centrality of the perceiver, that "hardest basic fact." It seems fair to conclude that certain of his critics have no grasp of physics or of metaphysics. In other words, in changing, our vocabulary has not always advanced.

Whitman was a Quaker and he wrote as one: "I say the real and permanent grandeur of these States must be their religion, / Otherwise there is just no real and permanent grandeur; / (nor character nor life worthy the name without religion . . .)." This is from *Leaves of Grass*, and so is this: "All parts away for the progress of souls, / All religion, all solid things, arts, governments, all that was or is / apparent upon this globe or any globe, / falls into niches and corners / before the procession of souls along / the grand roads of the universe." The vision of the soul, all souls, realizing itself in the course of transforming everything that has constrained it and them, finds expression in many writers of the period, prominent among them Emerson, Melville, and Dickinson, and in later writers such as William James and Wallace Stevens. For all of them creeds fall away and consciousness has the character of revelation. To identify sacred mystery with every individual experience, every life, giving the word its largest sense, is to arrive at democracy as an ideal, and to accept the difficult obligation to honor others and oneself with something approaching due reverence. It is a vision that is wholly religious though by no means sectarian, wholly realist in acknowledging the great truth of the centrality of human consciousness, wholly open in that it anticipates and welcomes the disruption of present values in the course of finding truer ones. And it is fully as well attested as America's old-time religion as is any exclusivist or backward-looking tradition, though our ill-informed nostalgias elevate what is called fundamentalism to that place, with the result that those who cannot endorse fundamentalist religion scorn the past while those who embrace it despise the present.

I have spent most of my life studying American history and literature. I have studied other histories and literatures largely to gain perspective on this civilization. The magnanimity of its greatest laws and institutions as well as its finest poetry and philosophy move me very deeply. I know that there are numberless acts of generosity, moral as well as material, carried out among its people every hour of the day. But the language of public life has lost the character of generosity, and the largeness of spirit that has created and supported the best of our institutions and brought reform to the worst of them has been erased out of historical memory. On both sides the sole motive force in our past is now said to have been capitalism. On both sides capitalism is understood as grasping materialism that has somehow or other yielded the comforts and liberties of modern life. Capitalism thus understood is seen on one side as providential, so good in its effects that it reduces Scripture with its do-unto-others to shibboleth. The other side sees it as more or less corrupting and contemptible but beyond human powers to resist.

And no one offers a definition of it. But in these days when its imperium is granted by virtually anyone who attends to such things, our great public education system is being starved and abandoned, and our prisons have declined to levels that disgrace us. The economics of the moment, and of the last several decades, is a corrosive influence, undermining everything it touches, from our industrial strength to our research capacity to the well-being of our children. I am not the first to suggest that it is undermining our politics as well.

What if good institutions were in fact the product of good intentions? What if the cynicism that is supposed to be rigor and the acquisitiveness that is supposed to be realism are making us forget the origins of the greatness we lay claim to—power and wealth as secondary consequences of the progress of freedom, or, as Whitman would prefer, Democracy? After all, these things rose together. The air is thick now with "the people," a phrase that is meant to give authority to the claims and the grievances of those who use it. That it is often invoked in good faith one may doubt, but the fact that resort is had to it so insistently means that we are still good enough democrats to feel that ultimately authority and reason do and should lie with the people. Then the old impulse that lay behind the dissemination of information and learning, the will to ensure that the public will be competent to make the weightiest decisions and to conform society to its best sense of the possible should be as powerful as it has ever been, and more powerful because of the fragility of the contemporary world. Instead we have slack and underfinanced journalism and the ebbing away of resources from our universities, libraries, and schools. The liberation of the human individual as a social value required optimism, which it also amply justified. This loyalty to democracy is the American value I fear we are gravely in danger of losing.

When I Was a Child
I Read Books

Freedom of Thought

Over the years of writing and teaching, I have tried to free myself of constraints I felt, limits to the range of exploration I could make, to the kind of intuition I could credit. I realized gradually that my own religion, and religion in general, could and should disrupt these constraints, which amount to a small and narrow definition of what human beings are and how human life is to be understood. And I have often wished my students would find religious standards present in the culture that would express a real love for human life and encourage them also to break out of these same constraints. For the educated among us, moldy theories we learned as sophomores, memorized for the test and never consciously thought of again, exert an authority that would embarrass us if we stopped to consider them. I was educated at a center of behaviorist psychology and spent a certain amount of time pestering rats. There was some sort of maze-learning experiment involved in my final grade, and since I remember the rat who was my colleague as uncooperative, or perhaps merely incompetent at being a rat, or tired of the whole thing, I don't remember how I passed. I'm sure coercion was not involved, since this rodent and I avoided contact. Bribery was, of course, central to the experiment and no black mark against either of us, though I must say, mine was an Eliot Ness among rats for its resistance to the lure of, say, Cheerios. I should probably have tried raising the stakes. The idea was, in any case, that behavior was conditioned by reward or its absence, and that one could extrapolate meaningfully from the straightforward demonstration of rattish self-interest promised in the literature, to the admittedly more complex question of human motivation. I have read subsequently that a female rat is so gratified at having an infant rat come down the reward chute that she will do whatever is demanded of her until she has filled her cage with them. This seems to me to complicate the definition of self-interest considerably, but complexity was not a concern of the behaviorism of my youth, which was reductionist in every sense of the word.

It wasn't all behaviorism. We also pondered Freud's argument that primordial persons, male, internalized the father as superego by actually eating the poor fellow. Since then we have all felt bad—well, the male among us, at least. Whence human complexity, whence civilization. I did better on that exam. The plot was catchy.

The situation of the undergraduate rarely encourages systematic doubt. What Freud thought was important because it was Freud who thought it, and so with B. F. Skinner and whomever else the curriculum held up for our admiration. There must be something to all this, even if it has only opened the door a degree or two on a fuller understanding. So I thought at the time. And I also thought it was a very bleak light that shone through that door, and I shouldered my share of the supposedly inevitable gloom that came with being a modern. In English class we studied a poem by Robert Frost, "The Oven Bird." The poem asks "what to make of a diminished thing." That diminished thing, said the teacher, was human experience in the modern world. Oh dear. Modern aesthetics. We must learn from this poem "in singing not to sing." To my undergraduate self I thought, "But what if I like to sing?" And then my philosophy professor assigned us Jonathan Edwards's *Doctrine of Original Sin Defended*, in which Edwards argues for "the arbitrary constitution of the universe," illustrating his point with a gorgeous footnote about moonlight that even then began to dispel the dreary determinisms I was learning elsewhere. Improbable as that may sound to those who have not read the footnote.

At a certain point I decided that everything I took from studying and reading anthropology, psychology, economics, cultural history, and so on did not square at all with my sense of things, and that the tendency of much of it was to posit or assume a human simplicity within a simple reality and to marginalize the sense of the sacred, the beautiful, everything in any way lofty. I do not mean to suggest, and I underline this, that there was any sort of plot against religion, since religion in many instances abetted these tendencies and does still, not least by retreating from the cultivation and celebration of learning and of beauty, by dumbing down, as if people were less than God made them and in need of nothing so much as condescension. Who among us wishes the songs we sing, the sermons we hear, were just a little dumber? People today—television—video games—diminished things. This is always the pretext.

Simultaneously, and in a time of supposed religious revival, and among those especially inclined to feel religiously revived, we have a society increasingly defined by economics, and an economics increasingly reminiscent of my experience with that rat, so-called rational-choice economics, which assumes that we will all find the shortest way to the reward, and that this is basically what we should ask of ourselves and—this is at the center of it all—of one another. After all these years of rational choice, brother rat might like to take a look at the packaging just to see if there might be a little melamine in the inducements he was being offered, hoping, of course, that the vendor considered it rational to provide that kind of information. We do not deal with one another as soul to soul, and the churches are as answerable for this as anyone.

If we think we have done this voiding of content for the sake of other people, those to whom we suspect God may have given a somewhat lesser brilliance than our own, we are presumptuous and also irreverent. William Tyndale, who was burned at the stake for his translation of the Bible, who provided much of the most beautiful language in what is called by us the King James Bible, wrote, he said, in the language a plowboy could understand. He wrote to the comprehension of the profoundly poor, those who would be, and would have lived among, the utterly unlettered. And he created one of the undoubted masterpieces of the English language. Now we seem to feel beauty is an affectation of some sort. And this notion is as influential in the churches as it is anywhere. The Bible, Christianity, should have inoculated us against this kind of disrespect for ourselves and one another. Clearly it has not.

For me, at least, writing consists very largely of exploring intuition. A character is really the sense of a character, embodied, attired, and given voice as he or she seems to require. Where does this creature come from? From watching, I suppose. From reading emotional significance in gestures and inflections, as we all do all the time. These moments of intuitive recognition float free from their particular occasions and recombine themselves into nonexistent people the writer and, if all goes well, the reader feel they know.

There is a great difference, in fiction and in life, between knowing someone and knowing *about* someone. When a writer knows *about* his character he is writing for plot. When he *knows* his character he is writing to explore, to feel reality on a set of nerves somehow not quite his own. Words like "sympathy," "empathy," and "compassion" are overworked and overcharged—there is no word for the experience of seeing an embrace at a subway stop or hearing an argument at the next table in a restaurant. Every such instant has its own emotional coloration, which memory retains or heightens, and so the most sidelong, unintended moment becomes a part of what we have seen of the world. Then, I suppose, these moments, as they have seemed to us, constellate themselves into something a little like a spirit, a little like a human presence in its mystery and distinctiveness.

Two questions I can't really answer about fiction are (1) where it comes from, and (2) why we need it. But that we do create it and also crave it is beyond dispute. There is a tendency, considered highly rational, to reason from a narrow set of interests, say survival and procreation, which are supposed to govern our lives, and then to treat everything that does not fit this model as anomalous clutter, extraneous to what we are and probably best done without. But all we really know about what we are is what we do. There is a tendency to fit a tight and awkward carapace of definition over humankind, and to try to trim the living creature to fit the dead shell. The advice I give my students is the same advice I give myself—forget definition, forget assumption, watch. We inhabit, we are part of, a reality for which explanation is much too poor and small. No physicist would dispute this, though he or she might be less ready than I am to have recourse to the old language and call reality miraculous. By my lights, fiction that does not acknowledge this at least tacitly is not true. Why is it possible to speak of fiction as true or false? I have no idea. But if a time comes when I seem not to be making the distinction with some degree of reliability in my own work, I hope someone will be kind enough to let me know.

When I write fiction, I suppose my attempt is to simulate the integrative work of a mind perceiving and reflecting, drawing upon culture, memory, conscience, belief or assumption, circumstance, fear, and desire—a mind shaping the moment of experience and response and then reshaping them both as narrative, holding one thought against another for the effect of affinity or contrast, evaluating and rationalizing, feeling compassion, taking offense. These things do happen simultaneously, after all. None of them is active by itself, and none of them is determinative, because there is that mysterious thing the cognitive scientists call self-awareness, the human ability to consider and appraise one's own thoughts. I suspect this self-awareness is what people used to call the soul.

Modern discourse is not really comfortable with the word "soul," and in my opinion the loss of the word has been disabling, not only to religion but to literature and political thought and to every humane pursuit. In contemporary religious circles, souls, if they are mentioned at all, tend to be spoken of as saved or lost, having answered some set of divine expectations or failed to answer them, having arrived at some crucial realization or failed to arrive at it. So the soul, the masterpiece of creation, is more or less reduced to a token signifying cosmic acceptance or rejection, having little or nothing to do with that miraculous thing, the felt experience of life, except insofar as life offers distractions or temptations.

Having read recently that there are more neurons in the human brain than there are stars in the Milky Way, and having read any number of times that the human brain is the most complex object known to exist in the universe, and that the mind is not identical with the brain but is more mysterious still, it seems to me this astonishing nexus of the self, so uniquely elegant and capable, merits a name that would indicate a difference in kind from the ontological run of things, and for my purposes "soul" would do nicely. Perhaps I should pause here to clarify my meaning, since there are those who feel that the spiritual is diminished or denied when it is associated with the physical. I am not among them. In his Letter to the Romans, Paul says, "Ever since the creation of the world [God's] invisible nature, namely, his eternal power and deity, has been clearly perceived in the things that have been made." If we are to consider the heavens, how much more are we to consider the magnificent energies of consciousness that make whomever we pass on the street a far grander marvel than our galaxy? At this point of dynamic convergence, call it self or call it soul, questions of right and wrong are weighed, love is felt, guilt and loss are suffered. And, over time, formation occurs, for weal or woe, governed in large part by that unaccountable capacity for self-awareness.

The locus of the human mystery is perception of this world. From it proceeds every thought, every art. I like Calvin's metaphor—nature is a shining garment in which God is revealed and concealed. As we perceive we interpret, and we make hypotheses. Something is happening, it has a certain character or meaning which we usually feel we understand at least tentatively, though experience is almost always available to reinterpretations based on subsequent experience or reflection. Here occurs the weighing of moral and ethical choice. Behavior proceeds from all this, and is interesting, to my mind, in the degree that it can be understood to proceed from it.

We are much afflicted now by tedious, fruitless controversy. Very often, perhaps typically, the most important aspect of a controversy is not the area of disagreement but the hardening of agreement, the tacit granting on all sides of assumptions that ought not to be granted on any side. The treatment of the physical as a distinct category antithetical to the spiritual is one example. There is a deeply rooted notion that the material exists in opposition to the spiritual, precludes or repels or trumps the sacred as an idea. This dichotomy goes back at least to the dualism of the Manichees, who believed the physical world was the creation of an evil god in perpetual conflict with a good god, and to related teachings within Christianity that encouraged mortification of the flesh, renunciation of the world, and so on.

For almost as long as there has been science in the West there has been a significant strain in scientific thought which assumed that the physical and material preclude the spiritual. The assumption persists among us still, vigorous as ever, that if a thing can be "explained," associated with a physical process, it has been excluded from the category of the spiritual. But the "physical" in this sense is only a disappearingly thin slice of being, selected, for our purposes, out of the totality of being by the fact that we perceive it as solid, substantial. We all know that if we were the size of atoms, chairs and tables would appear to us as loose clouds of energy. It seems to me very amazing that the arbitrarily selected "physical" world we inhabit is coherent and lawful. An older vocabulary would offer the word "miraculous." Knowing what we know now, an earlier generation might see divine providence in the fact of a world coherent enough to be experienced by us as complete in itself, and as a basis upon which all claims to reality can be tested. A truly theological age would see in this divine Providence intent on making a human habitation within the wild roar of the cosmos.

But almost everyone, for generations now, has insisted on a sharp distinction between the physical and the spiritual. So we have had theologies that really proposed a "God of the gaps," as if God were not manifest in the creation, as the Bible is so inclined to insist, but instead survives in those dark places, those black boxes, where the light of science has not yet shone. And we have atheisms and agnosticisms that make precisely the same argument, only assuming that at some time the light of science will indeed dispel the last shadow in which the holy might have been thought to linger. Religious experience is said to be associated with activity in a particular part of the brain. For some reason this is supposed to imply that it is delusional. But all thought and experience can be located in some part of the brain, that brain more replete than the starry heaven God showed to Abraham, and we are not in the habit of assuming that it is all delusional on these grounds. Nothing could justify this reasoning, which many religious people take as seriously as any atheist could do, except the idea that the physical and the spiritual cannot abide together, that they cannot be one dispensation. We live in a time when many religious people feel fiercely threatened by science. O ye of little faith. Let them subscribe to *Scientific American* for a year and then tell me if their sense of the grandeur of God is not greatly enlarged by what they have learned from it. Of course many of the articles reflect the assumption at the root of many problems, that an account, however tentative, of some structure of the cosmos or some transaction of the nervous system successfully claims that part of reality for secularism. Those who encourage a fear of science are actually saying the same thing. If the old, untenable dualism is put aside, we are instructed in the endless brilliance of creation. Surely to do this is a privilege of modern life for which we should all be grateful.

For years I have been interested in ancient literature and religion. If they are not one and the same, certainly neither is imaginable without the other. Indeed, literature and religion seem to have come into being together, if by literature I can be understood to include pre-literature, narrative whose purpose is to put human life, causality, and meaning in relation, to make each of them in some degree intelligible in terms of the other two. I was taught, more or less, that we moderns had discovered other religions with narratives resembling our own, and that this discovery had brought all religion down to the level of anthropology. Sky gods and earth gods presiding over survival and procreation. Humankind pushing a lever in the hope of aperiodic reward in the form of rain or victory in the next tribal skirmish. From a very simple understanding of what religion has been we can extrapolate to what religion is now and is intrinsically, so the theory goes. This pattern, of proceeding from presumed simplicity to a degree of elaboration that never loses the primary character of simplicity, is strongly recurrent in modern thought.

I think much religious thought has also been intimidated by this supposed discovery, which is odd, since it certainly was not news to Paul, or Augustine, or Thomas Aquinas, or Calvin. All of them quote the pagans with admiration. Perhaps only in Europe was one form of religion ever so dominant that the fact of other forms could constitute any sort of problem. There has been an influential modern tendency to make a sort of slurry of religious narratives, asserting the discovery of universals that don't actually exist among them. Mircea Eliade is a prominent example. And there is Joseph Campbell. My primary criticism of this kind of scholarship is that it does not bear scrutiny. A secondary criticism I would offer is that it erases all evidence that religion has, anywhere and in any form, expressed or stimulated thought. In any case, the anthropological bias among these writers, which may make it seem free of all parochialism, is in fact absolutely Western, since it regards all religion as human beings acting out their nature and no more than that, though I admit there is a gauziness about this worldview to which I will not attempt to do justice here.

This is the anthropologists' answer to the question, why are people almost always, almost everywhere, religious. Another answer, favored by those who claim to be defenders of science, is that religion formed around the desire to explain what prescientific humankind could not account for. Again, this notion does not bear scrutiny. The literatures of antiquity are clearly about other business.

Some of these narratives are so ancient that they clearly existed before writing, though no doubt in the forms we have them they were modified in being written down. Their importance in the development of human culture cannot be overstated. In antiquity people lived in complex city-states, carried out the work and planning required by primitive agriculture, built ships and navigated at great distances, traded, made law, waged war, and kept the records of their dynasties. But the one thing that seems to have predominated, to have laid out their cities and filled them with temples and monuments, to have es-

tablished their identities and their cultural boundaries, to have
governed their calendars and enthroned their kings, were the
vivid, atemporal stories they told themselves about the gods, the
gods in relation to humankind, to their city, to themselves.

I suppose it was in the eighteenth century of our era that
the notion became solidly fixed in the Western mind that all
this narrative was an attempt at explaining what science would
one day explain truly and finally. Phoebus drives his chariot
across the sky, and so the sun rises and sets. Marduk slays the
sea monster Tiamat, who weeps, whence the Tigris and the
Euphrates. It is true that in some cases physical reality is accounted for, or at least described, in the terms of these myths.
But the beauty of the myths is not accounted for by this theory,
nor is the fact that, in literary forms, they had a hold on the
imaginations of the populations that embraced them which
expressed itself again as beauty. Over time these narratives had
at least as profound an effect on architecture and the visual arts
as they did on literature. Anecdotes from them were painted
and sculpted everywhere, even on household goods, vases, and
drinking cups.

This kind of imaginative engagement bears no resemblance
whatever to an assimilation of explanatory models by these civilizations. Perhaps the tendency to think of classical religion as
an effort at explaining a world otherwise incomprehensible to
them encourages us to forget how sophisticated ancient people
really were. They were inevitably as immersed in the realm
of the practical as we are. It is strangely easy to forget that
they were capable of complex engineering, though so many of
their monuments still stand. The Babylonians used quadratic
equations.

Yet in many instances ancient people seem to have ob-
scured highly available real-world accounts of things. A sculp-
tor would take an oath that the gods had made an idol, after he
himself had made it. The gods were credited with walls and

ziggurats, when cities themselves built them. Structures of enormous shaped stones went up in broad daylight in ancient cities,
the walls built around the Temple by Herod in Roman-occupied
Jerusalem being one example. The ancients knew, though we
don't know, how this was done, obviously. But they left no account of it. This very remarkable evasion of the law of gravity
was seemingly not of great interest to them. It was the gods
themselves who walled in Troy.

In Virgil's *Aeneid*, in which the poet in effect interprets the
ancient Greek epic tradition by attempting to renew it in the
Latin language and for Roman purposes, there is one especially
famous moment. The hero, Aeneas, a Trojan who has escaped
the destruction of his city, sees a painting in Carthage of the
war at Troy and is deeply moved by it and by what it evokes, the
lacrimae rerum, the tears in things. This moment certainly
refers to the place in classical civilization of art that pondered
and interpreted the Homeric narratives, which were the basis
of Greek and Roman religion. My point here is simply that
pagan myth, which the Bible in various ways acknowledges as
analogous to biblical narrative despite grave defects, is not a
naive attempt at science.

It is true that almost a millennium separated Homer and
Virgil. It is also true that through those centuries the classical
civilizations had explored and interpreted their myths continuously. Aeschylus, Sophocles, and Euripides would surely have
agreed with Virgil's Aeneas that the epics and the stories that
surround them and flow from them are indeed about lacrimae
rerum, about a great sadness that pervades human life. The
Babylonian *Epic of Gilgamesh* is about the inevitability of death
and loss. This is not the kind of language, nor is it the kind of
preoccupation, one would find in a tradition of narrative that
had any significant interest in explaining how the leopard got
his spots.

The notion that religion is intrinsically a crude explanatory strategy that should be dispelled and supplanted by science is based on a highly selective or tendentious reading of the literatures of religion. In some cases it is certainly fair to conclude that it is based on no reading of them at all. Be that as it may, the effect of this idea, which is very broadly assumed to be true, is again to reinforce the notion that science and religion are struggling for possession of a single piece of turf, and science holds the high ground and gets to choose the weapons. In fact there is no moment in which, no perspective from which, science as science can regard human life and say that there is a beautiful, terrible mystery in it all, a great pathos. Art, music, and religion tell us that. And what they tell us is true, not after the fashion of a magisterium that is legitimate only so long as it does not overlap the autonomous republic of science. It is true because it takes account of the universal variable, human nature, which shapes everything it touches, science as surely and profoundly as anything else. And it is true in the tentative, suggestive, ambivalent, self-contradictory style of the testimony of a hundred thousand witnesses, who might, taken all together, agree on no more than the shared sense that something of great moment has happened, is happening, will happen, here and among us.

I hasten to add that science is a great contributor to what is beautiful and also terrible in human existence. For example, I am deeply grateful to have lived in the era of cosmic exploration. I am thrilled by those photographs of deep space, as many of us are. Still, if it is true, as they are saying now, that bacteria return from space a great deal more virulent than they were when they entered it, it is not difficult to imagine that some regrettable consequence might follow our sending people to tinker around up there. One article noted that a human being is full of bacteria, and there is nothing to be done about it.

Science might note with great care and precision how a new pathology emerged through this wholly unforeseen impact of

space on our biosphere, but it could not, scientifically, absorb the
fact of it and the origin of it into any larger frame of meaning.
Scientists might mention the law of unintended consequences—
mention it softly, because that would sound a little flippant in
the circumstances. But religion would recognize in it what religion has always known, that there is a mystery in human nature
and in human assertions of brilliance and intention, a recoil the
Greeks would have called irony and attributed to some angry
whim of the gods, to be interpreted as a rebuke of human pride
if it could be interpreted at all. Christian theology has spoken
of human limitation, fallen-ness, an individually and collec-
tively disastrous bias toward error. I think we all know that
the earth might be reaching the end of its tolerance for our
presumptions. We all know we might at any time feel the force
of unintended consequences, many times compounded. Science
has no language to account for the fact that it may well overwhelm itself, and more and more stand helpless before its own
effects.

Of course science must not be judged by the claims certain
of its proponents have made for it. It is not in fact a standard of
reasonableness or truth or objectivity. It is human, and has always been one strategy among others in the more general project of human self-awareness and self-assertion. Our problem
with ourselves, which is much larger and vastly older than science, has by no means gone into abeyance since we learned to
make penicillin or to split the atom. If antibiotics have been
used without sufficient care and have pushed the evolution of
bacteria beyond the reach of their own effectiveness, if nuclear
fission has become a threat to us all in the insidious form of a
disgruntled stranger with a suitcase, a rebuke to every illusion of
safety we entertained under fine names like Strategic Defense
Initiative, old Homer might say, "the will of Zeus was moving
toward its end." Shakespeare might say, "There is a destiny that
shapes our ends, rough-hew them how we will."

The tendency of the schools of thought that have claimed to be most impressed by science has been to deny the legitimacy of the kind of statement it cannot make, the kind of exploration it cannot make. And yet science itself has been profoundly shaped by that larger bias toward irony, toward error, which has been the subject of religious thought since the emergence of the stories in Genesis that tell us we were given a lavishly beautiful world and are somehow, by our nature, complicit in its decline, its ruin. Science cannot think analogically, though this kind of thinking is very useful for making sense and meaning out of the tumult of human affairs.

We have given ourselves many lessons in the perils of being half right, yet I doubt we have learned a thing. Sophocles could tell us about this, or the book of Job. We all know about hubris. We know that pride goeth before a fall. The problem is that we don't recognize pride or hubris in ourselves, any more than Oedipus did, any more than Job's so-called comforters. It can be so innocuous-seeming a thing as confidence that one is right, is competent, is clear-sighted, or confidence that one is pious or pure in one's motives. As the disciples said, "Who then can be saved?" Jesus replied, "With men this is impossible, but with God all things are possible," in this case speaking of the salvation of the pious rich. It is his consistent teaching that the comfortable, the confident, the pious stand in special need of the intervention of grace. Perhaps this is true because they are most vulnerable to error—like the young rich man who makes the astonishing decision to turn his back on Jesus's invitation to follow him, therefore on the salvation he sought—although there is another turn in the story, and we learn that Jesus will not condemn him. I suspect Jesus should be thought of as smiling at the irony of the young man's self-defeat—from which, since he is Jesus, he is also ready to rescue him ultimately. The Christian narrative tells us that we individually and we as a world turn our backs on what is true, essential, wholly to be desired. And it tells us that we can both know this about ourselves and forgive it in ourselves and one another, within the limits of our mortal capacities. To recognize our bias toward error should teach us modesty and reflection, and to forgive it should help us avoid the inhumanity of thinking we ourselves are not as fallible as those who, in any instance, seem most at fault. Science can give us knowledge, but it cannot give us wisdom. Nor can religion, until it puts aside nonsense and distraction and becomes itself again.

Imagination and Community

Over the years I have collected so many books that, in aggregate, they can fairly be called a library. I don't know what percentage of them I have read. Increasingly I wonder how many of them I ever will read. This has done nothing to dampen my pleasure in acquiring more books. But it has caused me to ponder the meaning they have for me, and the fact that to me they epitomize one great aspect of the goodness of life. Recently I bought a book titled *On What Cannot Be Said: Apophatic Discourses in Philosophy, Religion, Literature, and the Arts, Volume One: Classic Formulations.* The title itself is worth far more than the price of the book, and then there is the table of contents. So far I have read only the last and latest selection, from *The Wandering Cherub* by Silesius Angelus, who wrote in the seventeenth century.

In the stack of magazines, read and unread, that I can never bring myself to throw away, there are any number of articles suggesting that science, too, explores the apophatic—reality that eludes words—dark matter, dark energy, the unexpressed dimensions proposed by string theory, the imponderable strangeness described by quantum theory. These magazine essays might be titled "Learned Ignorance," or "The Cloud of Unknowing," or they might at least stand beside Plato's and Plotinus's demonstrations of the failures of language, which are, paradoxically, demonstrations of the extraordinary power of language to evoke a reality beyond its grasp, to evoke a sense of what cannot be said.

I love all this for a number of reasons, one of them being that, as a writer, I continuously attempt to make inroads on the vast terrain of what cannot be said—or said by me, at least. I seem to know by intuition a great deal that I cannot find words for, and to enlarge the field of my intuition every time I fail again to find these words. That is to say, the unnamed is over-whelmingly present and real for me. And this is truer because the moment it stops being a standard for what I do say is the moment my language goes slack and my imagination disen-gages itself. I would almost say it is the moment in which my language becomes false. The frontiers of the unsayable, and the avenues of approach to those frontiers, have been opened for me by every book I have ever read that was in any degree ambitious, earnest, or imaginative; by every good teacher I have had; by music and painting; by conversation that was in any way interesting, even conversation overheard as it passed between strangers.

As a fiction writer I do have to deal with the nuts and bolts of temporal reality—from time to time a character has to walk through a door and close it behind him, the creatures of imag-ination have to eat and sleep, as all other creatures do. I would have been a poet if I could, to have avoided this obligation to simulate the hourliness and dailiness of human life. This is not to say that books could not be written about walking through a door—away from what? toward what? leaving what wake of con-sequence? creating what stir of displacement? To speak in the terms that are familiar to us all, there was a moment in which Jesus, as a man, a physical presence, left that supper at Emmaus. His leave-taking was a profound event for which the supper it-self was precursor. Presence is a great mystery, and presence in absence, which Jesus promised and has epitomized, is, at a human scale, a great reality for all of us in the course of ordinary life.

I am persuaded for the moment that this is in fact the basis of community. I would say, for the moment, that community, at least community larger than the immediate family, consists very largely of imaginative love for people we do not know or whom we know very slightly. This thesis may be influenced by the fact that I have spent literal years of my life lovingly absorbed in the thoughts and perceptions of—who knows it better than I?—people who do not exist. And, just as writers are engrossed in the making of them, readers are profoundly moved and also influenced by the nonexistent, that great clan whose numbers increase prodigiously with every publishing season. I think fiction may be, whatever else, an exercise in the capacity for imaginative love, or sympathy, or identification.

I love the writers of my thousand books. It pleases me to think how astonished old Homer, whoever he was, would be to find his epics on the shelf of such an unimaginable being as myself, in the middle of an unrumored continent. I love the large minority of the writers on my shelves who have struggled with words and thoughts and, by my lights, have lost the struggle. All together they are my community, the creators of the very idea of books, poetry, and extended narratives, and of the amazing human conversation that has taken place across millennia, through weal and woe, over the heads of interest and utility.

We live on a little island of the articulable, which we tend to mistake for reality itself. We can and do make small and tedious lives as we sail through the cosmos on our uncannily lovely little planet, and this is surely remarkable. But we do so much else besides. For example, we make language. A language is a grand collaboration, a collective art form which we begin to master as babes and sucklings, and which we preserve, modify, cull, enlarge as we pass through our lives. Some students in

France drew my attention to the enormous number of English words that describe the behavior of light. Glimmer, glitter, glister, glisten, gleam, glow, glare, shimmer, sparkle, shine, and so on. These old words are not utilitarian. They reflect an aesthetic attention to experience that has made, and allows us to make, pleasing distinctions among, say, a candle flame, the sun at its zenith, and the refraction of light by a drop of rain. How were these words coined and retained, and how have they been preserved through generations, so that English-speaking people use them with the precision necessary to preserving them? None of this can be ascribed to conscious choice on the part of anyone, but somehow the language created, so to speak, a prism through which light passes, by means of which its qualities are arrayed. One of the pleasures of writing is that so often I know that there is in fact a word that is perfect for the use I want to put it to, and when I summon it it comes, though I might not have thought of it for years. And then I think, somewhere someone was the first person to use that word. Then how did it make its way into the language, and how did it retain the specificity that makes it perfect for this present use? Language is profoundly communal, and in the mere fact of speaking, then writing, a wealth of language grows and thrives among us that has enabled thought and knowledge in a degree we could never calculate. As individuals and as a species, we are unthinkable without our communities.

I remember once, as a child, walking into a library, looking around at the books, and thinking, I could do that. In fact I didn't do it until I was well into my thirties, but the affinity I felt with books as such preserved in me the secret knowledge that I was a writer when any dispassionate appraisal of my life would have dismissed the notion entirely. So I belong to the community of the written word in several ways. First, books have taught me most of what I know, and they have trained my attention and my imagination. Second, they gave me a sense of the possible, which is the great service—and too often, when it is ungenerous, the great disservice—a community performs for its members. Third, they embodied richness and refinement of language, and the artful use of language in the service of the imagination. Fourth, they gave me and still give me courage. Sometimes, when I have spent days in my study dreaming a world while the world itself shines outside my windows, forgetting to call my mother because one of my nonbeings has come up with a thought that interests me, I think, this is a very odd way to spend a life. But I have my library all around me, my cloud of witnesses to the strangeness and brilliance of human experience, who have helped me to my deepest enjoyments of it. Every writer I know, when asked how to become a writer, responds with one word: Read. Excellent advice, for a great many reasons, a few of which I have suggested here.

And this brings us to the subject of education. In the United States, education, especially at the higher levels, is based around powerful models of community. We choose our colleges, if we have a choice, in order to be formed by them and supported by them in the identities we have or aspire to. If the graft takes, we consider ourselves ever after to be members of that community. As one consequence, graduates tend to treat the students who come after them as kin and also as heirs. They take pride in the successes of people in classes forty years ahead of or behind their own. They have a familial desire to enhance the experience of generations of students who are, in fact, strangers to them, except in the degree that the ethos and curriculum of the place does indeed form its students over generations. These gifts are very often made, the donors say, out of gratitude and in celebration, and I have no reason to doubt it. I am even inclined to look charitably upon the fondness of donors for seeing their names on buildings and fountains, to consider it the expression of a desire to implant themselves immortally in the consciousness of a beloved community. In any case, many of our colleges and universities have been richly adorned over many years with assets and resources we are far too ready to take for granted. There are literally hundreds of places in this country where an open and committed student can enjoy an education that would be extraordinary by any except the very high standard so many of these institutions do sustain. This is not to devalue the achievements of any specific university, only to speak the pleasant truth about American higher education in general.

From time to time I, as a professor in a public university, receive a form from the legislature asking me to make an account of the hours I spend working. I think someone ought to send a form like that to the legislators. The comparison might be very interesting. The faculty in my acquaintance are quite literally devoted to their work, almost obsessive about it. They go on vacation to do research. Even when they retire they don't retire. I have benefited enormously from the generosity of teachers from grade school through graduate school. They are an invaluable community who contribute as much as legislators do to sustaining civilization, and more than legislators do to equipping the people of this country with the capacity for learning and reflection, and the power that comes with that capacity. Lately we have been told and told again that our educators are not preparing American youth to be efficient workers. Workers. That language is so common among us now that an extraterrestrial might think we had actually *lost* the Cold War.

The intellectual model for this school and for most of the older schools in America—for all of them, given the prestige and influence of the older schools—was a religious tradition that loved the soul and the mind and was meant to encourage the exploration and refinement of both of them. I note here that recent statistics indicate American workers are the most productive in the world by a significant margin, as they have been for as long as such statistics have been ventured. If we were to retain humane learning and lose a little edge in relative productivity, I would say we had chosen the better part. Since we need not choose between one or the other, I think we ought to reconsider the pressure, amounting sometimes to hostility, that has lately been brought to bear on our educational culture at every level, particularly in the humanities and the arts.

Here I have wandered into the terrain of societal tensions, by which the dear old United States is much afflicted at the moment. There is a notion with a brutal history that a homogeneous country is more peaceful and stable and, in a very deep sense, more satisfying than one with a complex and mingled population like ours. To an alarming extent, we have internalized this prejudice against ourselves. I have read that the word "heterogeneous," which was originally a term of geology, was first applied to society by the French writer Chateaubriand to describe America. Ironically, he was in America to escape the French Revolution and its aftermath, as thorough a social dissolution as has occurred in modern history. But he wrote that *America* was too *diverse* to be stable. Heterogeneous stone is not as solid as homogeneous stone. Oh, the power of metaphor.

In fact, Europe has gone berserk from time to time over this anxiety about mixed populations, most recently in the former Yugoslavia a few years ago. There is talk now that Belgium will cease to exist, having fallen into ethnic and linguistic halves, and there is fear that this will trigger divisions in other parts of Europe. This same anxiety is tormenting contemporary Africa, and it is one source of the disasters that have befallen Iraq. The assumption behind it is that people who differ from oneself are therefore enemies who have either ruined everything or are about to. It is the old assumption of Chateaubriand that difference undermines stability and strength.

When this assumption takes hold, the definition of community hardens and contracts and becomes violently exclusive and defensive. We have seen Christians against Christians, Muslims against Muslims, fighting to the death over distinctions those outside their groups would probably never notice and could certainly never understand. When definitions of "us" and "them" begin to contract, there seems to be no limit to how narrow these definitions can become. As they shrink and narrow, they are increasingly inflamed, more dangerous and inhumane. They present themselves as movements toward truer and purer community, but, as I have said, they are the destruction of community. They insist that the imagination must stay within the boundaries they establish for it, that sympathy and identification are only allowable within certain limits. I am convinced that the broadest possible exercise of imagination is the thing most conducive to human health, individual and global.

In fact, we in America have done pretty well. By human standards, which admittedly are low. That we have done relatively well, I submit, is due to the fact that we have many overlapping communities and that most of us identify with a number of them. I identify with my congregation, with my denomination, with Christianity, with the customs and institutions that express the human capacity for reverence, allowing for turbulence within these groups and phenomena. Since we are human beings, turbulence is to be expected. If the effect of turbulence is to drive me or anyone back on some narrower definition of identity, then the moderating effects of broader identification are lost. And this destroys every community—not only through outright suppression or conflict. Those who seemingly win are damaged inwardly and insidiously because they have betrayed the better nature and the highest teaching of their community in descending to exclusion, suppression, or violence. Those of us who accept a historical tradition find ourselves feeling burdened by its errors and excesses, especially when we are pressed to make some account of them. I would suggest that those who reject the old traditions on these grounds are refusing to accept the fact that the tragic mystery of human nature has by no means played itself out, and that wisdom, which is almost always another name for humility, lies in accepting one's own inevitable share in human fallibility.

I am a little sensitive on this point because another identification I hold passionately is with the academic community, which has its fair share of skeptics and agnostics, some of whom are well enough informed historically to mention Michael Servetus from time to time, to make an occasional offhand remark about the Thirty Years War. On all sorts of grounds I would go to the barricades to defend their right to make me uncomfortable, of course. They have caused me to ponder many things, to my great benefit. There are many examples now of friction between the extremes of these communities, and when it takes the form of radical opposition of either to the other the result is a decline from the humane standards that at best dignify them both. This university is an instance of the fact that they grew up together.

There are excitements that come with abandoning the constraints of moderation and reasonableness. Those whose work it is to sustain the endless palaver of radio and television increasingly stimulate these excitements. No great wonder if they are bored, or if they suspect their audiences might be. But the effect of this marketing of rancor has unquestionably been to turn debate or controversy increasingly into a form of tribal warfare, harming the national community and risking always greater harm. I think it is reasonable to wonder whether democracy can survive in this atmosphere. Democracy, in its essence and genius, is imaginative love for and identification with a community with which, much of the time and in many ways, one may be in profound disagreement.

Democracy wrote itself some interesting history in the second half of the last century. When I was in high school, there were essentially three choices available to a bright girl like myself. I could be a teacher, I could be a nurse, or I could be a homemaker. My chemistry teacher was so sure I would finally be a nurse that he gave me much better grades than I had earned, so that this path would not be closed to me. And my unknown in the final exam was sodium chloride. But my biology teacher noticed that my drawing of the frog we were supposed to have dissected was entirely too imaginative to reflect any acquaintance at all with the actual innards of the thing, and he, wisely, advised me to pay no attention to the chemistry teacher.

It was my brother who told me I should be a poet. This was not a career, as he or I understood it, but a highly respectable use of solitude. I never had any real aspiration, only the knowledge that adulthood would come and I would want to while it away harmlessly enough to be considered a credit to my family. This may not reflect well on me, but it's the truth, and I find it worth telling here because I was in fact pulled along into a broader and broader world by the generous interest of my brother, and of friends, a pastor, and various teachers. I believe I would have been happy with my unaspiring life—which always included a great deal of reading. But I am certain that I am happier with the very different, very interesting life that has befallen me.

When I was in college, at Pembroke, which has since disappeared into Brown, we women enjoyed exactly the same rigorous and ambitious education that the men did. Why? One dean explained to us that educated men preferred to have educated wives, and that corporations often interviewed the wife when they made decisions about whom to hire. Education made women socially presentable. This sounds appalling, but I don't think it was ever a real consideration for anyone. The faculty loved to teach, and they taught well, and a certain percentage of those they taught were women.

Just at that time the great social transformation began, set in motion by Rosa Parks, Martin Luther King, Jr., and many others, which called into doubt the whole system of discrimination that had governed most lives, not only in America but throughout the world. Almost suddenly an expanding field of possibility lay open to women, certainly to me. And almost as suddenly I had reasonable uses to make of my brains and my education. By chance I benefited profoundly from the self-transformation of communities and institutions that have been most central to my life. They changed my experience, and they also changed my mind. If I had lived a generation earlier, I might have thought about many of the things that interest me now, but not with the discipline that comes with writing about them or teaching, and not with the rigor that comes with being exposed to response and criticism. And, of course, I would have had no part in conversations that I consider important. So my mind has been formed by the uses I have been able to make of it. It is true for everyone that the experience that society gives to us, or denies us, is profoundly formative. Because I have lived at the cusp of great social change, I am perhaps especially aware of this fact. I am aware not only of the benefits I have enjoyed, sharing the life of this community, but also of the good service we can do one another by contributing as we can to the health, generosity, and courage of our community.

I have talked about community as being a work of the imagination, and I hope I have made clear my belief that the more generous the scale at which imagination is exerted,

the healthier and more humane the community will be.
There is a great deal of cynicism at present, among Americans, about the American population. Someone told me recently that a commentator of some sort had said, "The
United States is in spiritual free-fall." When people make
such remarks, such appalling judgments, they never include
themselves, their friends, those with whom they agree. They
have drawn, as they say, a bright line between an "us" and a
"them." Those on the other side of the line are assumed to be
unworthy of respect or hearing, and are in fact to be regarded
as a huge problem to the "us" who presume to judge "them."
This tedious pattern has repeated itself endlessly through human history and is, as I have said, the end of community and
the beginning of tribalism.

At this point in my life I have probably had a broader experience of the American population than is usual. I have been to
divinity schools, and I have been to prisons. In the First Epis-
tle of Peter we are told to honor everyone, and I have never
been in a situation where I felt this instruction was inappropriate. When we accept dismissive judgments of our community we stop having generous hopes for it. We cease to be capable
of serving its best interests. The cultural disaster called "dumbing down," which swept through every significant American
institution and grossly impoverished civic and religious life, was
and is the result of the obsessive devaluing of the lives that happen to pass on this swath of continent. On average, in the main,
we are Christian people, if the polls are to be believed. How is
Christianity consistent with this generalized contempt that
seems to lie behind so much so-called public discourse? Why
the judgmentalism, among people who are supposed to believe
we are, and we live among, souls precious to God—three hun-

dred million of them on this plot of ground, a population large and various enough to hint broadly at the folly of generalization? It is simply not possible to act in good faith toward people one does not respect, or to entertain hopes for them that are appropriate to their gifts. As we withdraw from one another we withdraw from the world, except as we increasingly insist that foreign groups and populations are our irreconcilable enemies. The shrinking of imaginative identification which allows such things as shared humanity to be forgotten always begins at home.

To look only at certain effects of this cynicism that manifest themselves in my experience: It is my good fortune to work with many gifted young writers. They are estimable people. The writers' workshop is as interesting and civilized a community as I have ever encountered, and it owes the successes of its long history to the fact that it works well as a community. A pretty large percentage of these fine young spirits come to me convinced that if their writing is not sensationalistic enough, it will never be published, or if it is published, it will never be read. They come to me persuaded that American readers will not tolerate ideas in their fiction. Since they feel that anything recognizable as an idea is off-limits to them, they sometimes try to signal intellectual seriousness by taking a jaundiced or splenetic view of the worlds they create and people. They are good, generous souls working within limits they feel are imposed on them by a public that could not possibly have an interest in writing that ignored these limits—a public they cannot respect.

Only consider how many things have gone wrong here, when a young writer is dissuaded by the pessimism that floats around the culture from letting her or his talent develop in the direction natural to it. If the writer is talented, the work might well be published, and the American reading public will look once more into the mirror of art and find sensationalism, violence, condescension, cynicism—another testament to collective mediocrity if not something worse. Maybe even spiritual free-fall. But the writer is better than this, and the reading public is better than this. And the publishing industry is better than this, too. The whole phenomenon is a mistake of the kind that is intractable because so much that passes for common wisdom supports it. A writer controlled by what "has" to figure in a book is actually accepting a perverse, unofficial censorship, and this tells against the writerly soul at least as surely as it would if the requirement being met were praise to some ideology or regime. And the irony of it all is that it is unnecessary and in many cases detrimental because it militates against originality. But the worst of it is that so long as a writer is working to satisfy imagined expectations that are extraneous to his art as he would otherwise explore and develop it, he is deprived of the greatest reward, which is the full discovery and engagement of his own mind, his own aesthetic powers and resources. So long as a writer is working below the level of her powers, she is depriving the community of readers of a truly good book. And over time a truly good book can enrich literally millions of lives. This is only one instance of the fact that when we condescend, when we act consistently with a sense of the character of people in general which demeans them, we impoverish them *and* ourselves, and preclude our having a part in the creation of the highest wealth, the testimony to the mysterious beauty of life we all value in psalms and tragedies and epics and meditations, in short stories and novels. In the same way we diminish the worth of the institutions of society—law, journalism, education, and religion as well, when we forget respect and love for the imagined other, the man or woman or child we will never know, who will take the good from these institutions that we invest in them, or who will be harmed or disheartened because our institutions are warped by meagerness and cynicism.

It is very much in the gift of the community to enrich individual lives, and it is in the gift of any individual to enlarge and enrich community.

The great truth that is too often forgotten is that it is in the nature of people to do good to one another.

Austerity as Ideology

Recently a friend sent me a composite photograph of the planet Mercury. Even as a composite, grossly disfigured to accommodate our strategies of perception, it had about it the great calm and sufficiency the ancients attributed to the spheres. The innumerable scars of eons of local cataclysm were only proof of its indomitability. Someone has named the more visible of these scars. The largest, a gigantic bloom of relative brightness, is Debussy. Machaut, Vivaldi, and Rachmaninoff have their craters; Rembrandt, Matisse, and Derain have theirs. And there is a fosse, a trench, called Pantheon, which I take to be a sort of shrine to the unknown, or in any case the unnamed, cultural gods. I like the eccentricity of the choices, which suggests that personal preferences are reflected in them. There is an astronomer somewhere who loves Machaut and Derain. So a record of his or her quietest human pleasures is inscribed, not on the planet, of course, but on its image. More detail has been added to our universe, to the map of what we know in the very human ways that we can know it.

The thought occurred to me that if the name of everyone on earth who is remembered for any kind of distinction were assigned to a crater or a mountain or a seeming rivulet somewhere in the visible universe, the astronomers would soon be out of names. The universe expands, in terms of the horizons of our awareness, in terms of its own phenomenal life, and again and most dramatically in terms of the horizons of plausible speculation. Indeed, these speculations involve the possibility of other universes preceding or coexisting with this one, in numbers that can fairly be called astronomical. Scatter the names of all those who have ever lived over the surface of the knowable cosmos, and it would remain, for all purposes, as unnamed as it was before the small, anomalous flicker of human life appeared on this small, wildly atypical planet.

Say that we are a puff of warm breath in a very cold universe. By this kind of reckoning we are either immeasurably insignificant or we are incalculably precious and interesting. I tend toward the second view. Scarcity is said to create value, after all. Of course value is a meaningful concept only where there is relationship, someone to do the valuing. If only to prove that I can, I will forbid myself recourse to theology and proceed as if God were not, for me, a given. Let us say that God is an unnecessary hypothesis here because we ourselves can value our own kind. There is perhaps nothing more startling about human circumstance than the fact that no hypothesis can be called necessary, that we are suspended in time ungrounded by any first premise, try as we may to find or contrive one.

We may say the human community can provide the nexus of relationship that makes the concept "value" meaningful. But evidence that this capacity is reliably present in us is not persuasive. Interdependency ought to ensure that we will regard one another as the basis of our own well-being, and will reciprocate, service for service, working out the fine points as circumstance requires. This has been a commonplace since antiquity. And it describes the ways of the gentle Tasaday, the dwellers in Utopia, certain religious orders and political movements while they are still drawing up charters and manifestos, and also certain villages and neighborhoods and exotic places as we remember or imagine them when the here and now is getting on our nerves. The logic of such mutuality and reci-

procity seems irrefutable, and so the falling short is always a
fresh surprise. Surely somewhere there are people still beyond
the reach of Western contact who live as nature would dictate.
But an anthropologist proceeding from another premise seems
always to have gotten to them first, and to have found them to
be the epitome of naturalness as he understands it, that is, xenophobic and homicidal. If we are a young species in evolutionary terms, we may well be old in terms of the span of life
our nature will allow us. And still we do not know what we are,
or why we act as we do.

This has always been as much a practical as a metaphysical
question, insofar as the two can be distinguished. Practically
speaking, we can persuade ourselves of anything at all and act
on it. This often manifests as a bold willingness to be rid of
problem populations—intellectuals, for example. Or Gypsies or
Cherokees or Albigensians or Carthaginians, or sturdy beggars,
or degenerates and social parasites. Anyone could add clearances
and pogroms and outright extirpations to this brief list. The
phenomenon recurs so often it should surely factor into any account we make of ourselves. Historical retrospect allows us to
identify with past victims, with their humanity, with the fact
that they were simply going about their lives and could not on
any reasonable grounds be blamed for the real or imagined
difficulties or the anticipated disasters that brought down real
calamity on them. We can admire whatever traces remain of
distinctive forms and motifs, we can retrieve the fragments of
poetry, and regret loss whose dimensions such remnants can
only suggest. Still, after so much history, those very irritations at
certain elements of society, certain problem populations, have
never gone away and are now clearly resurgent, becoming nor-
malized and respectable, as they have done so often in the past.

This teeming world, so steeped in its sins. No one could begin to count them. This does sound like theology of the darker
sort, the kind that would make us all inheritors not so much of

primal guilt as of a primal predisposition to incur guilt. We moderns are supposed to have liberated ourselves from such thinking. Belief in a bent toward acting badly has been taken to inhibit our potentiality for acting well, though why this should be true is not obvious. In any case, since we have behaved badly under both dispensations, we have provided ourselves with strong evidence for the soundness of the darker view—bad behavior for these purposes being defined as any act or omission, individual or collective, that diminishes human life. This standard might strike some as narrowly anthropocentric, but the interests of our species are so deeply intertwined with those of the planet that this definition should serve well enough.

And here we are. Wondering what this means, how we got where we are, it occurred to me to reread Winston Churchill's Iron Curtain speech. He called the speech "The Sinews of Peace," but whatever peaceable thrust it had seems to have been forgotten almost instantly, if it registered at all. Not surprisingly, given the times, and given the history of the world, it was an armed peace he had in mind. Clearly he wished to persuade his American audience that the British Empire would be strategically vital in a coming confrontation with an emerging Soviet adversary. His urging the importance of the Empire also seems to have made little impression, except, of course, on Stalin. But the Soviet threat, which was, formally at least, almost a subtext of the speech, had a profound, world-historical impact. Churchill said, "Not one country has slept less well in their beds because this knowledge [of the atomic bomb] and the method and the raw materials to apply it, are at present largely retained in American hands." But in 1946, when he spoke, Soviet scientists were known to be working desperately, sleeplessly, to bring an end to this monopoly, materially assisted by such notables as Donald Maclean and Klaus Fuchs. Churchill goes on to say, "I do not believe we should all have slept so soundly had the positions been reversed and some

Communist or neo-Fascist State monopolized for the time being these dread agencies. The fear of them alone might easily have been used to enforce totalitarian systems upon the free democratic world, with consequences appalling to human imagination."

Surely no Russian who read these words could have felt otherwise than threatened by them. To "appall human imagination" is no mean feat, after all. The American secretary of state and the British foreign minister both claimed, in the days that followed, not to have been aware of the contents of the speech before it was delivered. Churchill said truly that he spoke in a "sad and breathless moment." Any lover of mankind must regret that the world could not have caught its breath, healed, and rested a little before decisions were made that would shape and seal its future, as the perfection and deployment of these "dread agencies" have done. Stalin saw Churchill's vision of the role of the "English-speaking peoples" as equivalent to Hitler's vision of the role of the German-speaking peoples, that is, as their having by nature a right and obligation to control the future of the world. It must be said, he had a point. If, from a Western perspective, there were problems in the fact that the Soviets pursued Soviet policies in regions they controlled or influenced, it can hardly have come as a surprise. And Stalin's rationale for maintaining a Soviet empire, that it was necessary for defense, is entirely analogous to Churchill's rationale for maintaining a British empire.

Certainly there was an inevitable conflict of civilizations. But if the terms and conditions of the conflict had not been set at a time when the world was wounded and in shock, it might not have taken such destructive forms. It is important to remember that the American public learned about the atom bomb in the same moment the world learned about it. Though they had been entirely unconsulted in the matter of its use, as they had been in its creation, they could see the implications of both very clearly. Churchill alludes to the fact that America would not remain even relatively alone in the possession of this technology—he says it is in American hands "for the time being"—a point well calculated to encourage defensive anxiety by leveraging it against the horrors of the new warfare. This is a response Churchill is clearly ready to encourage. He says, "The dark ages may return, the Stone Age may return on the gleaming wings of science, and what might now shower immeasurable material blessings upon mankind, may even bring about its total destruction. Beware, I say; time may be short."

Granting the dangers of our moment, it is certainly questionable in a number of ways to conjure with the sense of crisis that swept the world during and after World War II, and especially to invoke the sense of existential threat with reference to carefully selected items in a national budget, or a perceived inadequacy of zeal in some part of a workforce. But this kind of language has become almost commonplace. Over the years we seem to have become habituated, even addicted, to the notion of radical threat, threat of the kind that can make virtually anything seem expendable if it does not serve an immediate, desperate purpose of self-defense—as defined by people often in too high a state of alarm to make sound judgments about what real safety would be or how it might be achieved, and who feel that their duty to the rest of us is to be very certain we share their alarm. Putting to one side the opportunities offered by the coercive power of fear, charity obliges me to assume that their alarm is genuine, though I grant that in doing so I again raise questions about the soundness of their judgment.

In this climate of generalized fear civil liberties have come under pressure, and those who try to defend them are seen as indifferent to threats to freedom. The world is indeed dangerous, and for this very reason the turning of our society, and of Western society, against themselves is flatly contrary to any rational strategy of self-defense. But it is highly consistent with a new dominance of ideological thinking, and it is very highly consistent with the current passion for Austerity, which gains from it status as both practical necessity and moral ideal. Anxiety has taken on a life of its own. It has become a sort of succubus on our national life.

A then probable candidate for the American presidency, Governor Mitch Daniels of Indiana, made a speech recently in which he said, "In our nation, in our time, the friends of freedom have an assignment as great as those of the 1860s, or the 1940s, or the long twilight of the Cold War. As in those days, the American project is menaced by a survival-level threat. We face an enemy, lethal to liberty, and even more implacable than those America has defeated before . . . I refer, of course, to the debts our nation has amassed for itself over decades of indulgence." Besides the recent financial crisis, which these thinkers always forget to mention, there is also the fact of our having indulged in two long and costly wars, and having indulged in taking up the novel burdens of security present circumstance requires. In such matters, securing nuclear sites, for example, it is easy to weigh the cost of what is done against the cost of failing to do it. A sound economics would apply this test in all cases. It would be harder then to rationalize Austerity, or to permit the onus of fiscal peril to be shifted onto the dependent and the vulnerable. Prominent political figures in America warn fairly often of economic holocaust, the destruction of all that has made us great, and a descent into the abyss of French-ness, even Greek-ness. Mutatis mutandis, presumably. Not Chinese-ness, though, which, by this mode of reckoning, ought to be a name for our aspirations.

A few days ago a British industrialist called for a new nationalism, the kind of spirit that prevails in time of war, to re-create Britain as a global economic power, which, in fact, it is already. In such a conflict the adversary is the relative economic success of another society. When this kind of competition is taken far enough, it can eventuate in literal warfare. Barring this, the quality of life on one side is sacrificed to the great work of depressing the quality of life on the other. Shooting war can usually rationalize itself in less desolate terms.

I grew up in the Cold War, in that long moment of anxious quiet called the Balance of Terror, the era of Mutually Assured Destruction, when the Iron Curtain was a dominant feature of life. We were taught to believe in the reality of an antagonism that might end in apocalypse. Apocalypse was not merely figurative language then, of course, and it is not now. But the nature of the antagonism was sometimes a little difficult to grasp. Each side proposed a way of life that was claimed to maximize human happiness. With all the problems the notion involves, we have come to a place where it would be tonic to hear that old phrase: the greatest good for the greatest number.

As children we were in fact encouraged to admire Russia, all those little Pioneers in their red scarves and very white shirts, their arms somehow always full of flowers, outdoing us in every measurable skill. I was led to believe that I and my peers were a slovenly lot who could never aspire to the first rank at anything—democracy and prosperity, those two great proofs of our superiority, were somehow deeply stultifying in their effects, so we were told. For this reason America was forever outskated, forever beaten at chess. Her youth would never truly master the violin. The twelve-year-old gymnasts of the Communist bloc would forever tie themselves in tighter knots than our twelve-year-old gymnasts. Their poets were treated by them as cultural treasures, while our poets, to the extent that they even deserved the name, loitered in a profound obscurity that served them right and still indicted the rest of us. I need not say how utterly Soviet youth outshone us at math and science, or how inevitably these attainments fed into the ever-increasing power and precision of their missiles, in tribute to which we sometimes crouched under our desks.

Human history is in large part nonsense, and I think it is appropriate to pay tribute to the percentage of the nonsense that is not tragic, that is harmless, even benign. Looking back at the challenges flung to us by the Soviets in our long struggle for hearts and minds, it is striking to realize how elegant, how courtly they tended to be. Their dancers and their skaters carried themselves like Romanovs, grave and unapproachable, aesthetically chaste and severe. It is striking as well how effectively their classicism governed the competition. Ballet was suddenly urgently important in America. Our orchestras were heroes of democracy for doing well just what they had always done. The Russians rejected modernism, and we looked a little askance at it ourselves, or flaunted it to the point of self-parody. Behind it all was an unspoken assumption carried on from the nineteenth century, that a great culture proved the health, worth, and integrity of a civilization. This was a sensitive issue for both countries, Russia having entered late into the Europe its arts so passionately emulated, America having entered late into existence as a nation. There are respects in which Russia was a good adversary. When they launched their first satellite, my little public school became more serious about my education. They helped to sensitize us to the hypocrisy of our position on civil rights, doing us a great service. This is not to minimize all that was regrettable, the doomsday stockpiles and that entrenched habit of ideological thinking, which lives on today among us, often in oddly inverted form, for example in the cult of Ayn Rand and the return of social Darwinism. The use of culture as proxy, its appropriation for political purposes, yielded a fair amount of self-consciousness and artificiality. Perhaps it compromised the authenticity of culture in ways that have contributed to the marginalization we see now. Still, given certain inevitabilities that beset the postwar world, the Russians were interesting and demanding of us, until our obsessions drifted elsewhere.

In the event, the competition between the United States

and the Soviet Union may indeed have been about economics. Or at least it seems to have come to an end on these grounds, if indeed it has finally ended. I know we capitalists are supposed to feel triumphant about this, and I may cause scandal by noting that the United States has had a long history of wealth and Russia a much longer history of poverty, that the United States built up its economy during World War II, while Russia suffered devastation. Perhaps I lament a readiness for competition that cannot acknowledge its advantage, now more common by the day. Graciousness might well be as appropriate, and emollient, in international relations as in other relations. Indeed, graciousness might be the most valuable consequence of objectivity. Russia fielded those soldiers of austere accomplishment, those concert pianists and chess masters, so effectively they allowed us to forget what for the world's sake we should have remembered, that we were inevitably perceived by them as an overwhelming threat.

I return to all these things on sleepless nights when I fall to wondering about the present state of my culture. I have always identified the United States with its best institutions and traditions, its best thought, believing, and having seen, that they could act as a corrective to the less admirable aspects of the culture. I have profoundly enjoyed the wealth of experience that has been offered to me, and I hope I have made some use of it. Yet it seems to me, on the darkest nights, and sometimes in the clear light of day, that we are now losing the ethos that has sustained what is most to be valued in our civilization. This may itself sound alarmist. But it is true, to paraphrase Franklin Roosevelt, that fear is very much to be feared, not least because it is a potent stimulant. Nothing is so effective at foregrounding self-interest. Yet fear is the motive behind most self-inflicted harm. Western society at its best expresses the serene sort of courage that allows us to grant one another real safety, real autonomy, the means to think and act as judgment and conscience dictate. It assumes that this great mutual courtesy will bear its best fruit if we respect, educate, inform, and trust one another. This is the ethos that is at risk as the civil institutions in which it is realized increasingly come under attack by the real and imagined urgencies of the moment. We were centuries in building these courtesies. Without them "Western civilization" would be an empty phrase.

In the contemporary world nothing of significance occurs in isolation. Austerity is the big word throughout the West these days, with the implicit claim that whatever the Austerity managers take to be inessential is inessential indeed, and that whatever can be transformed from public wealth into private affluence is suddenly an insupportable public burden and should and must be put on the block. Everywhere the crisis of the private financial system has been transformed into a tale of slovenly and overweening government that perpetuates and is perpetuated by a dependent and demanding population. This is an amazing transformation of the terms in which our circumstance is to be understood. For about ten days the crisis was interpreted as a consequence of the ineptitude of the highly paid, and then it transmogrified into a grudge against the populace at large, whose lassitude was bearing the society down to ruin. A few days ago, in Iowa, I saw a pickup truck with a bumper sticker that read DON'T DISTRIBUTE MY WEALTH. DISTRIBUTE MY WORK ETHIC. Iowa, as it happens, is famous for its work ethic, in a country whose attachment to work is so intense it is considered by some an affliction. But in the strange alembic of this moment, the populace at large is thought of by a significant part of this same population as a burden, a threat to their well-being, to their "values." There is at present a dearth of humane imagination for the integrity and mystery of other lives. In consequence, the nimbus of art and learning and reflection that has dignified our troubled presence on this planet seems now like a thinning atmosphere. Who would have thought that a thing so central to human life could prove so vulnerable to human choices?

Austerity has been turned against institutions and customs that have been major engines of wealth creation, because they are anomalous in terms of a radically simple economics. As a professor at a public university I feel the effects of this. Of course legislators are also state employees, but for the moment they are taken to act in the public interest when they attack the public sector. If they were to tell us taxpayers how they spend their time, fiscal demolition would account for a great part of it. The phenomenon is national, indeed global, since every entity with leverage on any other is bringing the same sort of pressure to bear. The countries we now call "developing" have dealt with this for many years—as often as the international financial institutions have decided that their economic houses need to be put in order. Their cultural and political integrity has been overridden whenever these agencies have invoked the supposedly unanswerable authority of economics. And now the West is seeing its own cultures and politics, indeed its modern social history, erased on these same grounds.

What has been achieved by these policies in the developing world may be open to debate. Prosperity and stability are creatures of definition and measurement, even when they appear to have been conjured out of insolvency, which is itself a creature of measurement and definition. It has been a matter of interest lately that Japan's debt is more than twice as large as its gross national product was before the country suffered disaster on March 11, 2011. If Japan were a developing country, this would certainly have been regarded as insolvency. But Japan is an important economy, so the same standards do not apply. Perhaps these standards, besides their being applied selectively, are suspect on other grounds. Japan has figured in the global economy as a major producer of wealth, no matter how dubious its financial arrangements—which were certainly rendered less dubious by the fact that no external agency would attempt to intervene in such an important economy.

It is this supranational power, Economics Pantocrator, that failed us all in fairly recent memory. It has emerged from the ashes with its power and its prestige enhanced even beyond the status it enjoyed in the days of the great bubble. The instability and the destruction of wealth for which it is responsible actually lend new urgency to its behests. This makes no sense at all. Certainly its authority with the public aligns badly with any conception of rational choice, which is supposedly a pillar of this selfsame economic theory. It can proceed confidently, and moralistically, in the face of common sense and painful experience because it *is* an ideology, the one we are supposed to believe was the champion of freedom and prosperity in the epic struggle called the Cold War. If there was such a champion, might it not have been freedom itself, as realized in the institutional forms of democracy? That is not how the story has been told. We are to believe it was an economic system, capitalism, that arrayed its forces against its opposite, communism, and rescued all we hold dear. Yet in the new era, market economics—another name for the set of theories and assumptions also called capitalism—has shown itself very ready to devour what we hold dear, if the list can be taken to include culture, education, the environment, and the sciences, as well as the peace and well-being of our fellow citizens.

Two things have happened more or less simultaneously. The world passed through a historic transformation associated with the computer and the Internet. This has been and will be a cause of profound economic and social disruption, and at the same time a great creator of wealth, a great enhancement of efficiency, and a great enrichment of life for those who have access to these resources and make good use of them. And then there is a separate development, the inscrutable financial economy abetted by the Internet, which has led to the over-valuing and then the collapse of basic elements of the traditional economy, notably pensions and real estate. Austerity policies, with the threat of worse to come, move people to put money in banks, or in investments they hope are safe, which no longer include the family home. If I cannot assume my adult children will have the pensions and benefits I enjoy, I will be much more inclined to make sure they have a good inheritance. This amounts to a fundamental reordering of American life. The wealth that was once frozen in appreciated value and thawed at the discretion of the owner, in homes, notably, is now, increasingly, liquid in the hands of international financial institutions. America has had a dynamic economy historically, one that grows and changes in ways that are difficult to anticipate. This no doubt reflects in part the broad distribution of wealth and education that have also characterized the country historically. This was conscious and intentional. Walt Whitman, writing after the Civil War, said, "The true gravitation-hold of liberalism in the United States will be a more universal ownership of property, general homesteads, general comfort, a vast, intertwining reticulation of wealth . . . A great and varied nationality . . . were firmest held and knit by the principle of the safety and endurance of the aggregate of its middling property owners." To project debt forward as the Austerity-mongers do is to assume a predictable future economy, essentially a zero-sum economy which can only increase wealth by depressing costs—wages, safety standards, taxes—that is to say, by moving wealth away from the general population. This prophecy will fulfill itself as education is curtailed and "reformed" to discourage intellectual autonomy, and so on. The new sense of insecurity, the awareness that the rules have suddenly changed, has a meaningful segment of the population furious at government and desperate to be rid of the institutions that enable a culture of innovation.

In any case, in America an abstraction called capitalism has truly begun to function as an ideology. The word is not included in the 1882 edition of Webster's dictionary, and in the latest *Oxford English Dictionary* capitalism is simply defined as "a system which favours the existence of capitalists," as the self-declared socialisms of Western Europe have always done. In contemporary America it has taken on the definition, and the character, Marx gave it, and Mao, and all the pro-Soviet polemicists. This despite the fact that Marx did not consider the United States of his time essentially capitalist. This despite the fact that the United States as a society is structured around any number of institutions that are not, under this definition, capitalist. Suddenly anything public is "socialism," therefore a deviancy, inevitably second-rate, and a corruption of, so to speak, the public virtue. If I could find any gleam of intelligence or reflection in all this, or any sign of successful education, I would be happy to admire it, so passionate are my loyalties. Failing this, I am left to ponder again the fact that this post-Soviet America has turned against its own culture and has seen cleavages in its own population that can only rejoice its most fervent ill-wishers. This is an ideal atmosphere for the flourishing of Austerity, punitive yet salvific, patriotic in its contempt for the thought and the values of those of its countrymen who have doubts as to its wisdom, especially if they express their doubts in the press or at the polls.

At very best there are two major problems with ideology. The first is that it does not represent or conform to or even address reality. It is a straight-edge ruler in a fractal universe. And the second is that it inspires in its believers the notion that the fault here lies with miscreant fact, which should therefore be conformed to the requirements of theory by all means necessary. To the ideologue this would amount to putting the world right, ridding it of ambiguity and of those tedious and endless moral and ethical questions that dog us through life, and that those around us so rarely answer to our satisfaction. Anger and self-righteousness combined with cynicism about the world as he or she sees it are the marks of the ideologue. There is always an element of nostalgia, too, because the ideologue is confident that he or she is moved by a special loyalty to a natural order, or to a good and normative past, which others defy or betray.

I am speaking of the troubled social and political environment in my own country, not because I think it is by any means alone in its confusions nor because I believe it is especially prone to them by the standards of other Western countries. It is simply the one culture about which I am competent to speak. At the same time, the march of Austerity, with all that means, is international. Historically there is nothing new about it. It is an assertion and a consolidation of power, capable of canceling out custom and social accommodation. It claims the force of necessity. And when necessity is to be dealt with, other considerations must be put aside. We in the West have created societies that, by historical standards, may be called humane. We have done this gradually, through the workings of our politics. Under the banner of necessity it can all be swept away.

The alienation, the downright visceral frustration, of the new American ideologues, the bone in their craw, is the unacknowledged fact that America has never been an especially capitalist country. The postal system, the land grant provision for public education, the national park system, the Homestead Act, the graduated income tax, the Social Security system, the G.I. Bill—all of these were and are massive distributions or redistributions of wealth meant to benefit the population at large. Even "the electrification of the countryside," Lenin's great and unrealized dream, was achieved in America by a federal program begun in 1936. Europeans are generally unaware of the degree to which individual state governments provide education, health care, libraries, and other services that complement or supplement federal programs, as do counties, cities, and other political entities. Since many American states are larger than many countries, their contributions are by no means inconsiderable.

These old and characteristic American arrangements do not fit well with a strict construction of the word "capitalist," as the neo-capitalists would understand it. They reflect nothing more ideological than consensus, varying among states and regions, about how best to "promote the general welfare," a role of the federal government stipulated in the preamble to the Constitution. These arrangements are pragmatic in nature, and therefore expressive of an effective freedom at odds with ideology. But the ideologues consider such things a straying from the true path. And who has led the march to decline? (Decline is a big concept, apparently based on the assumption that America, unlike every nation that has existed on earth, and despite its own history, will never have grave problems to deal with, except those that portend a fall into the everlasting dustbin. So any problem can be seen as grounds for outright panic or at best apocalyptic gloom.) But who is to blame? The government, of course, especially when it is run by Democrats, and by Republicans who now and then act like Democrats.

And this brings me back to the subject of competition, that great ally of Austerity. There is the ancient habit of competition between nations—for the biggest fleet, for access to commodities, for colonies, for the technologies of warfare. Even cultural competition is ancient—for example, the Roman desire for an epic to compare with Homer's. I know Americans are supposed to believe in competition. I think it is wasteful and undignified in most cases.

Our competition with the Russians, insofar as it was cultural, was harmless to moderately beneficial. Insofar as it was military, it was disastrous for both sides. I am speaking of those stockpiles and everything that has gone into the making of them. But the story that has currency is that we *competed* with the Russians and we *won*. So there is a heightened and ongoing zeal for competition, without a continental power on the other side of the earth to dignify the role of competitor. Since September 11, 2001, some have attempted to put radical Islam in the place of Godless communism. But the Muslim world is too diverse, too important to Western interests, too indifferent to the Tchaikovsky competition and speed skating to fill the role. In need of the focus that comes with having an alien and threatening government to contend against, a considerable number of Americans now choose to consider their own government alien and threatening, and, for good measure, Socialist. Again, this kind of thinking is eminently compatible with Austerity, since the redistributive activities of government are exactly what they choose to be austere about. Other alternatives would include returning tax rates for the very wealthy to historically typical levels and cutting subsidies to oil companies. Or there could be a candid admission that the responsibilities of the government involve it in great expense. None of these options ignites populist zeal. This is reserved for attacks—call them austerities—directed toward public schools, Social Security, national health care, the laws that protect air and water quality.

Stripped of all these burdens, America will be able to "compete." As will Greece and Portugal, I suppose. With whom? For what? China comes to mind. And economic preeminence. But China has in many ways already achieved the radical capitalism our ideologues still only dream of. Extreme Austerity is its starting place. It has cheap labor, an absence of environmental and workers' protections, and a demonstrated gift for capital accumulation, which it uses to position itself globally. A great part of this capital is Western, our civilization betting against itself, even stacking the cards, but never mind. An enormous population with a rising standard of living, engaged in the world economically as the Soviet Union never was, and creating dependency in the West as the Soviet Union never did is inevitably a global power. If it enjoys a healthy evolution and its people become more prosperous and freer, with greater access to the benefits of the wealth they create, this, objectively considered, will be an excellent thing for the human species, which is so largely Chinese.

In the best case such a China will overshadow the dear old West in important ways, presumably. In the worst case, it will become another adversary, and the potential for desperate and devastating great power frictions will be realized, testing the endurance of the habitable world yet again, and more severely. I would like to see the cost of these contests monetized, as they say. I know I speak very hypothetically when I say that nuclear plants might be built on the cheap, *designed* to operate for thirty years and *built* to last until their shoddiness is a problem that can no longer be ignored. A great deal of money changes hands, industries hum for a while. And what is the long-term cost when things go wrong? These reactors might, again hypothetically, be built in countries eager to take their place among the producers of export products that must, by every means, be made competitive—that is, far cheaper than they ought to be.

How should we reckon cost? And how do we reckon debt? Iowa, my adopted state, has a relatively small population and an economy based on agriculture. This has described the place for as long as it has been a name on a map. Iowa also has a fine system of public universities, which represent many generations of support from the people of Iowa, now more often called the taxpayers, so schooled have we been lately in thinking of our investments as exactions. Especially in the Midwest, state universities are flagship institutions, sources of pride and identity. They are virtual city-states, distinctive and autonomous. They carry on every kind of scholarship and research at the highest levels. Historically they have offered education at modest cost to the people whose support has created them and have opened their formidable resources to the public freely. Someone seems to have noticed that this sort of thing is not, under the strict new definition, capitalist. Something so valuable as education should be commodified, parceled up, and sold. The inefficiency of profit should be added, as a sort of tribute to this economic truth. The word "elite," or "elitist," has currency these days. Its connotations are bitterly negative in some circles. Universities and those who are associated with them are considered elitist, and this somehow disqualifies them morally for positions of public trust. But the whole point of the land grant system has been to create an elite so large the name no longer serves, to create a ruling class that is more or less identical with the population. To raise tuitions and exclude on economic grounds is the kind of "reform" that will create elitism of the very worst kind.

And how do we reckon ownership? Who owns these institutions? The generations who first broke ground for them? Who saw them through wars and depressions, when the wealth of this present generation would still have been unimaginable? My university is more than 150 years old. It was built on generosity and good faith. Why should all these hundreds of little farm towns sustain such a thing? They have sustained it heroically. Who should own its resources and its reputation? They are very valuable, so there is money to be squeezed out, certainly. There are corporations ready to rent it or buy it piecemeal. It is as if the very idea of a people, a historical community, has died intestate, and all its wealth is left to plunder.

This is simply to put in concrete terms questions of wealth and debt and ownership. Those in earlier generations who intended the benefits of education for me did not intend them any less for my great-grandchildren. But the new ideology seems to assume that the public as such cannot legitimately own anything or obligate the living to anything—for example, to providing the same access to education we have enjoyed. Education is associated with prosperity, so there is every reason to assume our shortfall can be monetized in reduced prosperity for our children or grandchildren. This will of course make more onerous the burden of debt the party of Austerity is always telling us we will leave them, dooming the poor souls to a future yet more Greek. If we educate them well, we give them the means to create a future that we cannot anticipate. If we cheat them, they will have the relatively meager future we have prepared for them. If Mozart is good for the brain in utero, it is no doubt good for the brain in middle age. And so with culture generally, which provides us with the paradigms of thought.

What are we doing here? We may never know. If a solar storm should burn off the peculiar damp that clings to this planet, this would be a very small change—no change at all in cosmic terms, which apparently are based on averages. The universe is lifeless now and will be lifeless then, so negligible is our presence in it. What about us was of interest, if we imagine looking at ourselves in retrospect? That we made civilizations, or that we drove them to the ground, reduced them to rubble? I won't pretend that this is a real question. We make wealth, and we destroy it. Our wealth is finally neither more nor less than human well-being. There is no necessary hypothesis, there is no value but what we value. The great temptation of money is that it seems to give us tokens, markers, by which things and people can be truly said to succeed or fail. The illusion that value inheres in it has vigorously survived a recent proof of its evanescence, in fact its utter dependency on our faith in its value. It has a placebo effect more predictably than it ought to, seeming to satisfy a need to know how value is discovered, or created, or conveyed, or preserved. It is human nature to want to know this. But whatever else we might say about human nature, we can say it aligns most inexactly with the universe.

In this moment the habit of aggressive fear and the zeal for Austerity have become a binary system, each intensifying the force of the other as they become a single phenomenon. In the way of the cosmically accidental, this near fusion has occurred at a point in time when the merely possible took on the character of the inevitable.

To put it another way, we have entered into a period of rationalist purgation. Rationalism and reason are antonyms, the first fixed and incurious, the second open and inductive. Rationalism is forever settling on one model of reality; reason tends toward an appraising interest in things as they come. Rationalism projects, and its projections typically fill it with alarm because of the inadequacy of its model, which, to the rationalist mind, appears as the perversity of the world. To this mind every problem is systemic, therefore vast and urgent. Rationalism is the omnium-gatherum of resentment and foreboding, the omnium-scatterum of everything of any kind that appears to stand in the way of a correction of reality back toward rational standards. Like paranoia, it all makes perfect sense, once its assumptions are granted. Again, like paranoia, it gathers evidence opportunistically, and is utterly persuaded by it, fueling its own confidence, sometimes to the point of messianic certainty. Ideology is rational, a pure product of the human mind.

There is an old saying: Act in haste and repent at leisure. Perhaps we understand this in an inverse and diabolical sense. We may actually enjoy repenting. We make it one of the more strenuous of our leisure occupations, especially when we feel we are repenting for crimes that are only "ours" in the broadest sense. But—oddly enough—we repent from the perspective of the victim, which we may have acquired only on our own terms and from a comfortable distance. Words such as "sympathy" and "compassion" encourage identification with the victim. But moral rigor and a meaningful concern for the future of humankind would require that we identify instead with the villain, while villainy is still only potential, while we can still try to ensure that we would not, actively or passively, have a part in it. It would require that we forbid ourselves to hope the offense will soon be over, the journalists will find something else to talk about. Then we will once again have leisure to repent the neglect and abuse that has receded into the past far enough to let us, in our heart of hearts, feel the most attenuated guilt, the kind made tolerable by our knowing that only a very delicate conscience would pause over it. Those factories that run on the labor of children, filling our world with so many attractive products that are really much cheaper than they ought to be—have they gone away? No, but our attention has wandered, and that is the next best thing from the point of view of our spiritual comfort. From the point of view of our material comfort, it is quite certainly the best thing.

There is a case to be made for the idea that we human beings create the universe in the fact of perceiving it, since it exists as we know it only because we bring particular abilities and limitations to the problem of knowing anything. Science tells us we came to the universe very recently, after a great deal of important business had been transacted here, the emergence of light and matter, for example. It would be interesting to know how so much that eludes our understanding and perception could be in any sense dependent on them. Still, we are that mysterious presence, the Observer, who can never wholly stand apart from the object of inquiry. If the consensus of the global population created the universe, it would differ very substantially from the one given us by the little clutch of mathematicians at the frontiers of the question. I suspect we would find it a stiflingly crude and lumpish little cosmos, if meaningful in its way. Some nostalgia has been devoted to the loss by us moderns of the conception of the universe that put humankind at its physical center, or at least did not overwhelm us so utterly with its power and scale. But the universe of the mathematicians, however important its departures may, over time, prove to be from an objectively existing universe, is unspeakably beautiful. I should be more specific. The universe that they manage to capture, however tentatively, out of the totality of phenomena is magnificent for the aura of implication that surrounds it, the tantalizing not-yet-knowable and the haunting never-to-be-known.

And there is a much larger, more general sense in which we are creators of the universe. We would not be the first human beings to base a universe on fear, and to make sacrifices to allay it which seem unaccountable from the perspective of another culture or generation. We can channel and exploit minds and energies, bending them to use against imagined adversaries. These things have been done any number of times. The alternative is to let ourselves be—that is, to let ourselves be the reflective, productive creatures we are, unconstrained and uncoerced. Eliminate the overwhelming cost of phantom wars and fools' errands, and humankind might begin to balance its books.

After all, its only debts are to itself.

Open Thy Hand Wide: Moses and the Origins of American Liberalism

In the famous address titled "The Genteel Tradition in American Philosophy," delivered in California in 1911, George Santayana said, "America is a young country with an old mentality: it has enjoyed the advantages of a child carefully brought up and thoroughly indoctrinated; it has been a wise child. But a wise child, an old head on young shoulders, always has a comic and an unpromising side. The wisdom is a little thin and verbal, not aware of its full meaning and grounds; and physical and emotional growth may be stunted by it, or even deranged." This "old head" on America's shoulders, he says, is Calvinism. Santayana does acknowledge that he is using this word in a special sense, one which allows him to find Calvinism in the Koran and in Cardinal Newman. He says,

> Calvinism, taken in this sense, is an expression of the agonised conscience. It is a view of the world which agonised conscience readily embraces if it takes itself seriously, as, being agonised, of course it must. Calvinism, essentially, asserts three things: that sin exists, that sin is punished, and that it is beautiful that sin should exist to be punished. The heart of the Calvinist is therefore divided between tragic concern at his own miserable condition, and tragic exultation about the universe

at large. He oscillates between a profound abasement and a paradoxical elation of the spirit. To be a Calvinist philosophically is to feel a fierce pleasure in the existence of misery, especially of one's own, in that this misery seems to manifest the fact that the Absolute is irresponsible or infinite or holy.

And so on.

This kind of invective against Calvinism is characteristic of the period, to be found in D. H. Lawrence, John Dalberg Acton, H. L. Mencken, Hilaire Belloc, Jacques Maritain, and, in slightly muted form, Max Weber. I quote at length—and I could quote at still greater length—because here Santayana's argument jumps the track. It is as if the mere word "Calvinism," redefined by him to mean a certain kind of unlikable excess wherever in the world it might be discovered or imagined, triggers an outpouring of stereotyped language. This denunciation is typical in that it offers no particulars about any teaching of Calvin's, and no example of Calvinistic philosophy. There is a certain poignant pleasure in learning that Americans were once faulted for an excess of gentility and even for a precocious wisdom, but there is nothing wise or philosophical, or, for that matter, genteel, about the mentality as he goes on to describe it. Still, I believe he is right in saying "the country was new, but the race was tried, chastened, and full of old memories," that it was "an old wine in new bottles." But the wine was older than Calvinism, than Christianity itself. It was what Jesus of Nazareth called the good old wine of Moses (Luke 5:39).

The status of the Old Testament in the Calvinist tradition has been used polemically against it, just as Calvinism has been used polemically against the Old Testament. Adolf Harnack wrote, in his *Marcion: The Gospel of the Alien God*, that in the Calvinist churches,

the Old Testament that was placed on a fully equal
footing with the New Testament had an unhealthy effect on dogmatics, on piety, and on the practice of the
Christian life. In some groups it even produced an Islamic zeal, while in others it called forth a new kind of
Judaism and promoted everywhere a legalistic entity . . .
If Marcion had reappeared in the time of the Huguenots and Cromwell, he would once again have encountered the warlike God of Israel whom he abhorred,
right in the very middle of Christendom. A reaction
was bound to come, and it arose in the very territories of
that Christianity—Calvinist Christianity—in which
the spirit of the Old Testament had so unthinkingly
been granted room.

Of course Oliver Cromwell, whatever his faults, can hardly be
said to compare badly with Philip II of Spain, or with any
number of Christian enthusiasts who preceded him, and who
took up a very New Testament sword of the Lord. That equiv-
alencies of this kind are so available in Christian history is a
somber truth by now acknowledged on every side, only slightly
mitigated by the fact that they are equally available in pagan
history. Certainly World War I, just ended when Harnack's
book appeared in 1920, exceeded the worst depredations of
Cromwell, Philip II, or "the warlike God of Israel." But it is
typical of modern disparagement of the Old Testament to assume a superior posture, as if we had put all thought of enormity far behind us.

Harnack's treatise on Marcion is in effect an appreciation
of this first great Christian heretic, whom Harnack compares
to Martin Luther. I am aware that Harnack's very confident
account of Marcion and his heresy is written at a far greater
remove from its subject than any Gospel account of Jesus, and

that Harnack is inevitably as much or more my subject than the heretic himself. So whatever I say about Marcion should be understood as a paraphrase of Harnack. This only makes the book more germane as an instance of the modern life of an ancient polemic. Marcion's doctrine, according to Harnack, simply carried to a logical conclusion the opposition between grace and works, the spirit and the law, to be found in the letters of Paul. This meant the rejection by Marcion of the Old Testament and the purging of the New Testament of books and passages he took to have been compromised by Jewish influences and interpolations. When he was done rather little remained. To his purged canon he appended a book of his own called *Antitheses*, which placed teachings of the Old and the New Testaments in opposition in order to demonstrate their radical unlikeness.

It is unfortunate that this book has not survived, since the assumption behind it, that the Testaments are at best incompatible, is with us still, though no one seems to feel any need now to make the case. It is usual to see the Old Testament treated as a sort of dead weight on Christianity, if not a positive embarrassment to it, by scholars as well as clergy. For this reason the text is very little studied or taught, except to dismantle its narratives on what are claimed to be critical grounds or to loot it for those few verses that seem to endorse condemnations Jesus himself did not engage in. So the Marcionist view of it as a crude document profoundly at odds with the gospel of grace becomes more and more entrenched, even in the Reformed or Calvinist tradition for whose theology it was once central.

Be that as it may. According to Harnack, the reaction to the prominence of the Old Testament takes place "first of all in the English Enlightenment." He cites Thomas Morgan, an Anglican clergyman and author of *The Moral Philosopher: A Dialogue Between Philalethes a Christian Deist, and Theophanes a Chris-*

tian Jew, published in 1737. In it, Harnack says, paraphrasing Morgan,

> The God of the Old Testament is pictured, approximately as Marcion had done, as a limited, petty, and contradictory national deity who also does immoral things; the Mosaic legislation is a wholly unsatisfactory, particularly limited and offensive work, a distortion of the *lex naturae*, very little different from the pagan religions. The nation of Israel, of bad character from the outset, runs aground on this law. Jesus brings the *lex naturae* that is clarified by means of revelation; Paul was his only true disciple; all the other disciples misunderstood Jesus and fell back into the Jewish way; along with them the church also fell, and thus . . . down to the present time it is halfway snared in Judaism.

This is a further polemical association, not a surprising one to find in a book written in early twentieth-century Europe, by a scholar so well respected even as Harnack. Then again, there is nothing except its expressed contempt for Judaism to distinguish this characterization of "the Old Testament God" from the commonplaces of recent scholarship and quasi-scholarship.

According to Harnack, Marcion's "alien god" or "unknown god" is a deity superior to the God of Moses, aloof from creation and from humankind through all the ages until his abrupt intervention in the rarefied person of Christ. The appeal of all this as a way of disburdening Christianity of its origins in Judaism is clear. This is a task some Christians have worked at since Marcion and no doubt before him, always with more than a little success. Though we live in an atmosphere of self-declared ecumenism, the polemic against the Hebrew Bible has become as if substance and settled truth.

Our modern Marcionism lacks the ancient metaphysical rigor. Still, moved by a dualist impulse that undermines the authority of the Hebrew Bible, we have conjured a sort of demiurge of our own, a being we call Yahweh. However sound the scholarship that lies behind this voicing of the divine name—a presumption in itself—it is associated with a reductionist and disparaging view of "the Old Testament God." The pious among us embrace a notion of Christ that sets him apart from, or against, this very improbable Father of his, adjusting to an inevitable loss of meaning of fine old words such as "incarnation," and to a contraction and impoverishment of our sense of the created order, which can hardly reflect the glory of a deity who is himself not especially glorious. This grim little perplex is often embraced as "liberalism" because it has an aura of learnedness about it, and modernity, though in essence it is very old indeed.

This success comes at a cost for all Christianity that Harnack and others never choose to acknowledge. This same hermeneutics has been brought to bear on the New Testament, predictably. More important from a Christian point of view, it has come at the cost of a model for true social justice and an ethos to support it. For the Calvinist or Reformed tradition, the effective exclusion of the Old Testament as a fully equal presence in the Christian canon has had profoundly disabling consequences. Contrary to entrenched assumption, contrary to the conventional associations made with the words "Calvinist" and "Puritan," and despite the fact that certain fairly austere communities can claim a heritage in Reformed culture and history, Calvinism is uniquely the *fons et origo* of Christian liberalism in the modern period, that is, in the period since the Reformation, and this liberalism has had its origins largely in the Old Testament. This is a bold statement, very much against the grain of historical consensus. Though I acknowledge that it may be indefensible in any number of particulars, I will argue that in a general sense it is not only true but a clarification of history important to contemporary culture and to that shaken and diminishing community, liberal Protestantism.

I know I am stepping into a semantic quagmire. Harnack himself is called a "liberal" theologian and historian, in the very influential sense the word acquired when the project of dismantling the traditional canon was still relatively new and somewhat controversial. The fact that words have different meanings in different cultures, that "liberal" is itself a word with very different meanings in American and European contexts, for example, never seems to influence discussion as it ought to. It is surely significant that the word is used in American discourse from the seventeenth century with insistent reference to scriptural contexts in which it occurs, while in England it is adopted from nineteenth-century French and has first of all a political connotation associated with the French Revolution, at least according to the *Encyclopaedia Britannica*. But in Renaissance French, *liberal, liberalité* meant "generous," "generosity," and of course the word occurs in the English Puritan translations, the Matthew's Bible and the Geneva Bible, which were followed in their use of the term by the 1611 Authorized Version.

The word occurs in contexts that urge an ethics of non-judgmental, nonexclusive generosity. Isaiah 32:6–8 in the 1560 Geneva Bible reads as follows: "The nigarde shal no more be called liberal, nor the churl riche. But the nigarde wil speake of nigardnes, and his heart wil worke iniquitie, and do wickedly, and speake falsely against the Lord, to make emptie the hungrie soule, and to cause the drinke of the thirstie to faile. For the weapons of the churl are wicked: he diviseth wicked counsels, to undo the poore with lying wordes: and to speake against the poor in judgement. But the liberal man wil divise of liberal things, and he wil continue his liberalitie." The Wycliffe Bible, which was translated from the Latin Vulgate, renders the last verse this way: "Forsoothe a prince schal thenke tho thingis

that ben worthi to a prince, and he shal stonde over duykis."
(Forsooth, a prince shall think those things that be worthy to
a prince, and he shall stand over dukes.) The New Jerusalem
Bible in English is closer to Wycliffe and Jerome: "the noble
person plans only noble things, / noble his every move." The
New International Version has "the noble man makes noble
plans, and by noble deeds he stands." This tradition of translation conveys a sense that an aristocratic virtue and obligation
is being praised here.

Calvin had important support among the French and European nobility, but he was no admirer of the institution. In his
Commentary on Genesis he interprets verse 6:4, "There were giants
in the earth in those days," as describing the origins of aristocracy. He says, "[U]nder the magnificent title of heroes, they
cruelly exercised dominion, and acquired power and fame for
themselves, by injuring and oppressing their brethren. And
this was the first nobility of the world. Lest any one should too
greatly delight himself in a long and dingy line of ancestry,
this, I repeat, was the nobility, which raised itself on high, by
pouring contempt and disgrace on others." It is no cause for
wonder that Calvin chose to democratize a virtue that was so
central to his piety and his teaching. He clearly did not consider "nobility" a synonym for "generosity."

It is interesting to note certain differences between Jerome's
Latin and Calvin's. Jerome's *insipiens*, "foolish," becomes Calvin's
sordidus, "base" or "vile." *Fraudulentus*, "deceitful," becomes *parcus*,
"sparing" or "frugal"; *stultus*, "foolish," becomes *sordidus*, "vile"; and
fraudulenti, "deceitful," becomes *avari*, "covetous" or "greedy." In
Calvin's reading the text is both harsher and more pointedly relevant to an ethic of generosity. The word *nigarde* in the English
of the Geneva Bible has an unpleasant sound but only one
meaning—it refers to stinginess. The interpretation offered in
the Geneva Bible derives from Calvin's Latin translation from

the Hebrew and his gloss of it. In Calvin's Latin, verse 32:8 reads: "*At liberalis liberalia agitabit, et liberaliter agendo progredietur.*" He says, "This relates ... to the regenerate, over whom Christ reigns; for, although all are called by the voice of the gospel, yet there are few who suffer themselves to be placed under his yoke. The Lord makes them truly kind and bountiful, so that they no longer seek their own convenience, but are ready to give assistance to the poor, and not only do this once or oftener, but every day advance more and more in kindness and generosity."

Contrary to popular opinion, Calvin says it is a misreading of the verse to think it means "that the liberal advance themselves, and become great by doing good; because God rewards them, and bestows on them greater blessings." On the contrary, they advance in an increasing liberality: "[T]rue liberality is not momentary or of short duration. They who possess that virtue persevere steadily, and do not exhaust themselves in a sudden and feeble flame, of which they quickly afterwards repent." As he does always, Calvin forbids any narrowing of the obligation of generosity. He says, "There are indeed many occurrences which retard the progress of our liberality. We find in men strange ingratitude, so that what we give appears to be ill bestowed. Many are too greedy, and, like horse-leeches, suck the blood of others. But let us remember this saying, and listen to Paul's exhortation 'not to be weary in well-doing;' for the Lord exhorts us not to momentary liberality, but to that which shall endure during the whole course of our life." Again, Calvin understands the passage to refer not to an aristocratic virtue but to a Christian imperative. In fact he sees the judgment of Christ present in the words of the Prophet: "In this passage, therefore, we are brought to the judgment-seat of Christ, who alone, by exposing hypocrisy, reveals whether we are covetous or bountiful."

The Geneva Bible has this for Deuteronomy 15:13–14, a law that specifies the way in which a freed servant is to be dealt

with: "And when thou sendest him out fre from thee, thou shalt
not let him go away emptie, but shalt give him a liberal rewarde
of thy shepe, & of thy corne, and of thy wines: thou shalt give
him of that wherewith the Lord thy God hathe blessed thee."
There is a marginal note that explains this as justice to the
worker: "In token that thou . . . acknowledge the benefite which
God has given thee by his [the worker's] labours." In the
Wycliffe Bible the verses read this way: "And thou shalt not suf-
fre hym to go away voide, to whom thou hast givve fredom; but
thou schalt give lijflode in the weye, of flocks, and of corn-
floor." In the Douay-Rheims, "[Thou] shall give him his way
out of thy flocks," and so on. Having no Hebrew, I look to the
Jewish Publication Society translation to umpire these differences, and I find that their version is closer to Jerome and
Wycliffe than to the Reformers. They have, "Furnish him out
of the flock"—there is no mention of a "liberal reward." In a
sermon on this text, Calvin says, "[A]ccording to your abilitie
you be bound to recompense them that have travelled for you,
& have bin the instruments of such blessings. For if we thank
God with our mouthes, confessing that it is he which hath
blessed us, & in the mean while make none account of such as he
has sent to doe us service in the increase of our living, by taking
paynes and toyle for us; all our thanking of him is but lip-labor &
utter hypocrisy." For Calvin, every human encounter is of moment, the other in the encounter is always "sent" or "offered." So
respect for every circumstance is reverence to God. Here is the
Geneva version of Deuteronomy 15:11: "Because there shal be
ever *some* poore in the land, therefore I commande thee, saying,
Thou shalt open thy hand unto thy brother, to thy nedie, and to
thy poore in thy land." This more or less agrees with other translations. There is, however, a note in the margin: "Thou shalt be
liberal."

When all is said and done, the word "liberal" and its forms
occur only a few times, even in the classic Protestant translations.

Their five occurrences in the King James Version of the Old Testament translate three different Hebrew words, suggesting that the translators were moved rather than required to make use of them. "Blessing," "voluntary," "to fit out with supplies"—if my concordance can be trusted, these are alternative translations of the words translated as "liberal" or "liberally" or "liberality." Translation is always interpretation in some degree, and, for those who, like Calvin and the classic Calvinists, take the Old Testament to be a revelation of God, or, to use a word almost interchangeable for Calvin, of Christ, then the spirit of law and prophecy are faithfully rendered, whatever questions might arise as to the letter. All this is of interest because the verses I have quoted, and the word "liberal" itself, supported by the meaning the verses give to it, are central to American social thought from its beginning.

Like old Israel, the United States is often said to be legalistic. And for some reason this is taken to be a criticism and to identify a failing. It might better be thought of as an acknowledgment of the human propensity to sin or error, in tension with an active solicitude for human vulnerability to the effects of sin and error, the two embraced by an unusual awareness, as self-created and intentional societies, of a calling to be "good" societies. When Americans launched on the project of national formation, there was still plenty of old wine in those new bottles.

In Old Testament monotheism uniquely it is humankind who introduce evil into the created order, that same humankind who are made in the image of God and whom God loves. This great paradox has the effect of centering the problem of evil in human nature and human choice. More precisely, the concept appears to arise not from any desire to escape or contain the complexities of the problem of evil but from a sense of

the literally cosmic significance of humankind as a central ac-
tor in creation who is, in some important sense, free to depart
from, even to defy, the will of God. Again paradoxically, the
very magnitude of the problem of evil is the reflex of human
centrality, because of the weight it gives to our presence in the
world and because only we among creatures are capable of the
concept. This vision of human nature and divine nature raises
more questions than it answers, in part because it does not
localize or personify evil. By the standards of other ancient
myth, it yields a kind of realism, an attention to mingled lives
and erring generations that grounds sacred meaning very solidly in this human world.

Israel's extraordinarily high valuation of life in the world
and in community led naturally to the centrality of law. "Law"
is a word that has had a special place in Christian thought on
the basis of certain understandings of Paul's use of it. For Harnack, at least in his interpretation of Marcion, it means the
opposite of grace. That is, it runs contrary to the will of God,
incurring misapprehension of the kind that is not only erring but
damnable. Like most Christian commentators, Harnack never
pauses to sort through the varieties of teaching or instruction
that are called "law," though for him they are for all purposes of
one kind with the most precisian of the Levitical laws.

Many of the laws attributed to Moses pertaining to social
order and social ethic have theological force because he, unlike
Hammurabi, Lycurgus, and Solon, was a religious founder as
well as a lawgiver in the usual sense. The eighteenth-century
Englishman Thomas Morgan objects to the laws on the grounds
that they pertain only to social order, which in his view precludes their having any higher meaning. In *The Moral Philosopher*, quoted above, he says, "[T]he reasons of this weakness and
insufficiency of the moral law, as delivered by Moses, are very
obvious. For, as this law was barely civil, political or national,
so all its sanctions were merely temporal, relating only to men's

outward practice and behaviour in society" and therefore "could not relate to the inward principles or motives of action, whether good or bad, and therefore could not purify the conscience, regulate the affections, or correct and restrain the vitious desires, inclinations and dispositions of the mind."

Only the tradition of Moses integrated civil law into the religious mythos, the sacred narrative. For this reason it has the singular inflection of an attentive, passionate—and singular— divine voice. In what other body of law could compliance be urged with the phrase "for you know the heart of the stranger"? This is not to minimize the ethical achievements of great pagans like Plato and Cicero, achievements revered by Christians for as long as the classics were read and there were still Christians of a mind to revere. But the extreme tension these pagans felt between the traditions of Hesiod and Homer and their own ethical systems is well known and very much to the point.

Some fragments of the Twelve Tablets of Roman Law survive. They are part of a social code, and might suggest something of the character of civil law in an earlier period, nearer to the time of Moses. Two laws respecting the treatment of debtors are of particular interest in light of the attention paid to this question in the Pentateuch. One says: "If they (creditor and debtor) do not come to another agreement, debtors are held in bonds for sixty days. During that time they are brought before court on three successive market days, and the amount for which they are liable shall be publicly announced." And the next says: "On the third market day [any multiple] creditors shall cut [the debtors] into pieces. If they shall cut more or less than their due, it shall be with impunity."

As with any ancient law, including those attributed to Moses, it is possible to say that this doesn't mean what it seems to mean, or it wasn't really enforced. And to make this kind of argument is perfectly respectable so long as it is made even-handedly. That said, over against this language, it is striking to note how protective, even tender, comparable Old Testament laws are toward debtors. This is Deuteronomy 24:10–13: "When you make your neighbor a loan of any sort, you shall not go into his house to fetch his pledge. You shall stand outside, and the man to whom you make the loan shall bring the pledge out to you. And if he is a poor man, you shall not sleep in his pledge; when the sun goes down, you shall restore the pledge that he may sleep in his cloak and bless you; and it shall be righteousness to you before the Lord your God." The Geneva Bible has a note that makes the law gentler yet. It says, "As though ye wouldst appoint what to have, but shalt receive what he may spare." No one can read the books of Moses with any care without understanding that law can be a means of grace. Certainly this law is of one spirit with the Son of Man who says, "I was hungry and you fed me. I was naked and you clothed me." This kind of worldliness entails the conferring of material benefit over and above mere equity. It means a recognition of and respect for both the intimacy of God's compassion and the very tangible forms in which it finds expression. Cranky old Leviticus gave us—gave Christ—not only "Thou shalt love thy neighbor as thyself" but also the rather forgotten "Thou shalt love the stranger as thyself," two verses that appear to be merged in the Parable of the Good Samaritan. Still, startlingly gentle laws like these fall under the general condemnation of Old Testament severity, and Calvin's refinements with them.

The tendency to hold certain practices in ancient Israel up to idealized modern Western norms is pervasive in much that passes for scholarship, though a glance at the treatment of the great class of debtors now being evicted from their homes in America and elsewhere should make it clear that, from the point of view of graciousness or severity, an honest comparison is not always in our favor. Morgan is right about the this-worldliness of the Torah, and wrong in suggesting that this must mean its teachings are therefore without transcendent mean-

ing. "Do unto others" is a behest that, if acted on, can have very
tangible, real-world consequences. The emperor Julian notes
that no Jew is ever forced to beg. So this-worldly are God's
interests that he cares whether some beleaguered soul can find
comfort in his sleep. He cares even to the point of overriding
what are called by us, though never by Moses or Jesus, the rights
of property.

Sir Thomas More, in his *Utopia*, published in Latin in 1516,
mentions this in the context of the forced depopulations of the
English countryside that were leading to mass destitution and
therefore rampant theft, which was answered by hanging. His
Raphael Hythlodaeus says, "Under the law of Moses—which
was harsh enough in all conscience, being designed for slaves,
and rebellious ones at that—thieves were not hanged, but merely
fined. We can hardly suppose that the new dispensation, which
expresses God's fatherly kindness towards His children, allows
us more scope than the old for being cruel to one another." In
the Christian Europe of the sixteenth century—or, for that matter, the nineteenth century—it would have been wholly appropriate to apply Origen's test of direct comparison of the laws of
Moses to prevailing law to determine which of them should be
called harsh.

Consistent with the polemical treatment of Old Testament
law is the equally polemical approach to American Puritan culture, which was indeed influenced in a remarkable degree by
this law. A code published in 1641 called *The Massachusetts Body of
Liberties* makes this clear. It is often compared to the Magna
Carta, to which it in fact bears little resemblance. A notable
feature of the code is a list of twelve infractions for which the
punishment is death. In each of them, and for them only, the
penalty is justified, or perhaps required, by citations from Exodus, Leviticus, Numbers, or Deuteronomy. One may not worship another god, practice witchcraft, blaspheme, commit willful
murder, murder in rage, poison, have relations with an animal,

have relations with another man, commit adultery, steal some-one, or bear false witness in a capital case. A twelfth, unbibli-cal law forbids any attempt to overthrow the commonwealth. By the standards of the period this code is remarkable in that it does not even mention property crime as a capital offense. The capital crimes are the kind of thing for which we would find any society of the period stern or intolerant. But these laws, like the laws of Moses, do not foresee that the poor will be made first beggars, then thieves, and then corpses, as Thomas More said of British law.

Where the *Liberties* depart from biblical example, they are compromised by habits of mind the colonists had not yet un-learned. Number 43 stipulates that "No man shall be beaten with above 40 stripes." Deuteronomy 25:3 says, "Forty strypes shal [the judge] cause him to have and not past, lest he shulde excede and beate him above that with manie stripes, thy brother shulde appeare despised in thy sight." Again that haunting so-licitude for the vulnerable, even one made vulnerable by his own transgression. And solicitude as well for one who risks the sin of despising his brother. The second clause of the colonists' law reads "nor shall any true gentleman, nor any man equall to a gentleman be punished with whipping, unles his crime be very shamefull, and his course of life vitious and profligate." This adaptation draws attention to the absence of such dis-tinctions of class in Moses's law. That said, it is instructive to compare the Massachusetts *Liberties* with the Grand Model for North Carolina, drawn up by John Locke at the request of the king and published in 1663, which would have established landed aristocracy and virtual feudalism in that colony.

According to the Massachusetts code,

Every person within this Jurisdiction, whether inhab-itant or forreiner shall enjoy the same justice and law,

that is general for the plantation . . . If any servants
shall flee from the Tiranny and crueltie of their masters to the howse of any freeman of the same Towne,
they shall be there protected and susteyned till due
order be taken for their relife . . . If any man smite out
the eye or tooth of his man-servant or maid servant, or
otherwise mayme or much disfigure him, unlesse it be
by meere casualtie, he shall let them goe free from his
service . . . No man shall exercise any Tiranny or Crueltie towards any bruite Creature which are usuallie
kept for man's use . . . No man shall be put to death
without the testimony of two or three witnesses or
that which is equivalent thereunto . . . For bodilie
punishments we allow amongst us none that are inhumane Barbarous or cruel.

These are all drawn from the laws of Moses, to be realized again
in early Massachusetts. They were not by any means in effect
universally in the thirteen colonies or the early United States.
That the same reforms were emerging in contemporary British law is unsurprising, since Puritanism was on the rise there,
reaching the point of revolution and an attempted social reordering. They were in some degree contravened in Massachusetts after the Cromwell period, when British authority over
the colony could be more effectively asserted.

That the teaching and example of Calvin were a great influence on Puritan culture and political thought is a commonplace,
of course—the words "Puritan" and "Calvinist" are virtually
interchangeable, and the harshness associated with both words
is taken to be the predominant feature of the societies they
created. In crowded, besieged, and turbulent Geneva, severity
might be expected and perhaps even excused. Yet on the subject of beggars and how begging is to be eliminated, though

Calvin says, like Thomas More, "To be shorte, of Roges, they become robbers, & in the end what must become of that?," his argument then takes a characteristic turn.

> But yet howsoever the case stand, let us see that the poore be mainteined. For if a man forbid begging, & therewithal doe no almes at all it is as much as if he did cut the throtes of those that are in necessitie. Nay, we must so provide for the poore, and redresse their want, that such as are stout beggers and apparently seeme not to be pitied, may be reformed. For they doe but eate up the others bread, & rob the needy of that which should be given unto them. That (say I) in effect, is the thing we have to marke here. But how may it be done? First, the Hospitals shoulde provide wel for such needs... [L]et not men play the good husbands in hording up the things that ought to be bestowed upon God & upon those whome he offreth unto us. Also as every man knoweth the particular needs of his neighbors, so let him indevour to succor them, and consider where wante or neede is, and helpe to remedie it. If this be done, then shal beggerie be taken away as it ought to be, and they shall not neede to make a simple forbidding of it; saying, let not men beg any more; & in the meane season the poore be left destitute, to die for hunger & thirst.

Calvin says, "[A]lthough a man cannot set downe a Lawe certeine in this behalfe; yet must every man be a rule to himselfe, to do according to his own abilitie and according to the need that he seeth in his neighbors." This is from a sermon on Deuteronomy delivered in French in 1555.

Like the New Englanders, Calvin shows the influence of his time and culture, tending in certain ways and degrees to modify the liberalism of Moses—for example, interpreting as respite from debt the laws that called for outright forgiveness and release. Nevertheless there is a striking generosity in his approach to the problem of theft, by the standards of his time and of ours. The provisions for the poor which structure both land ownership and the sacred calendar in ancient Israel, the rights of gleaners and of those widows, orphans, and strangers who pass through the fields, and the cycles of freedom from debt and restoration of alienated persons and property, all work against the emergence of the poor as a class, as people marked by deprivation and hopelessness. There is no sense of fearful urgency, there are no special measures to suppress crime driven by need except, as Calvin clearly understands, the preemption of crime through the alleviation of need.

In his *Institutes of the Christian Religion*, Calvin establishes a profound theological basis for liberality, openhandedness. He says,

> The Lord commands us to do "good unto all men," universally, a great part of whom, estimated according to their own merits, are very undeserving; but here the Scripture assists us with an excellent rule, when it inculcates, that we must not regard the intrinsic merit of men, but must consider the image of God in them, to which we owe all possible honour and love; but that this image is most carefully to be observed in them "who are of the household of faith," inasmuch as it is renewed and restored by the spirit of Christ. Whoever, therefore, is presented to you that needs your kind offices, you have no reason to refuse him your assistance. Say he is a stranger; yet the Lord has impressed on him a character which ought to be familiar to you; for which reason he forbids you to despise your own flesh. Say that he is contemptible and worthless; but the Lord shows him

to be one whom he has deigned to grace with his own image. Say that you are obliged to him for no services; but God has made him, as it were, his substitute, to whom you acknowledge yourself to be under obligations for numerous and important benefits. Say that he is unworthy of your making the smallest exertion on his account; but the image of God, by which he is recommended to you, deserves your surrender of yourself and all that you possess. If he not only deserved no favour, but, on the contrary, has provoked you with injuries and insults,—even this is no just reason why you should cease to embrace him with your affection, and to perform to him the offices of love. He has deserved, you will say, very different treatment from me. But what has the Lord deserved? who, when he commands you to forgive all men their offences against you, certainly intends that they should be charged to himself.

These are the consequences for Christians of the great teaching reiterated in Genesis, that every human being is an image of God, and it is another exploration of the unqualified requirement of generosity to be found in Deuteronomy 15. This more than reconciles Law and Gospel. It makes the two indistinguishable. And it makes trivial any attempted distinction between the this-worldly and the transcendent.

The early New Englanders, or those who defined and led the communities they established, are conventionally described as Calvinists. In fact their history and influence are almost always interpreted consistently with the popular characterization of Calvinism, almost always without significant reference to Calvin's theology, which does in fact pervade their thought. Though it is true that he is seldom referred to by them, they are Calvin's heirs in nothing more than in their refusal to argue from any authority but Scripture. Even Jonathan Edwards cites the great reformer only in a context in which he takes issue with him. The argument is made, when note is taken of the incompatibility of Calvin's own teaching with the kind of thinking ascribed to his influence, that there was an intervening "Calvinism," properly called so even though it departed radically from or was flatly contrary to his teaching. "Calvinism" in this second sense is the major term in Max Weber's unaccountably influential interpretation of the modern world, the same "Calvinism" Santayana found in the Koran, or perhaps I should say the "Koran," since, as both Santayana and Harnack demonstrate, this text and its culture also fall within the circle of things used polemically against each other.

In "A Modell of Christian Charity," his address aboard the *Arabella* to Puritans newly arrived in Massachusetts in 1630, John Winthrop makes an argument for liberality and bounteousness that follows the rhetorical strategy of objection and answer used by Calvin in the passage from the *Institutes* quoted above. A century before Winthrop spoke, William Tyndale's translation of the New Testament had replaced the word "charity" with the word "love," a change that was both valid as a correction and also full of ethical and theological implications. Winthrop's text in fact proceeds through a series of arguments in favor of charity as the word is ordinarily understood, to a celebration of the experience of love, which overrides all the considerations of need and worthiness on the one hand and of cost or sacrifice on the other, considerations that make it painful to give and more painful to receive, that together have given charity a bad name, precisely because complacency or condescension or contempt seem so often to have displaced love altogether.

Winthrop begins his argument by granting that, indeed, through the providence of God, "in all times some must be rich, some poore." This is true, he says, because God counts himself "more honoured in dispensing his gifts to man by man, than if he did it by his owne immediate hands." In other words, God is to be honored in the sharing of his gifts. The existence of rich and poor may be ordained as the condition of mankind, but for Winthrop this does not mean, as it has often been interpreted to mean, that an order ordained by God must be preserved by human effort and determination, especially when these are so powerfully supported by what Scripture assures us are our baser motives. We are not required to bring in the tide or to send the moon through its phases—a good thing, since we would surely find a way to default. We can, however, increase and embitter poverty. The prophets inform us of the Lord's views on that subject.

Like Calvin, Winthrop says that natural law "propounds one man to another, as the same flesh and Image of God." He says, "The Lawe of nature would give no rules for dealing with enemies, for all are to be considered as friends in the state of innocency, but the Gospell commands love to an enemy." He urges his hearers to accept that unlimited generosity might sometimes be required of them by particular "seasons and occasions." He says "community of perils calls for extraordinary liberality" and we must sometimes help the distressed "beyond our ability rather than tempt God in putting him upon help by miraculous or extraordinary means." Solomon offers arguments to "persuade to liberality." Referring to Deuteronomy 15, he says that we must lend freely and forgive the debts of those who cannot repay them. "Observe againe that the Scripture gives no caussion to restrain any from being over liberall this way; but all men to the liberall and cherefull practise hereof by the sweeter promises." And love, true charity, transcends all the considerations that make even liberality measured and conditional. "Shee [Love] setts noe boundes to her affections, nor hath any thought of reward. Shee findes recompense enough in the exercise of her love towardes [its object]." Like Calvin, Winthrop proposes a "modell of Christian Charity" based largely on the teaching of the Old Testament, that urges a literally unconditional generosity or, to use his word, liberality. This address, which must be very little read, has nothing of the prophetic triumphalism our politicians have claimed to find in it. As "a city on a hill," Winthrop says, the colony's failures will be conspicuous and notorious. He says that if they "shall fall to embrace this present world and prosecute our carnall intentions, *seeking greate things for ourselves and our posterity* [emphasis mine] the Lord will surely breake out in wrathe against us." And "if our heartes shall turne away, soe that wee will not obey, but shall be seduced and worshipp and serve other Gods, *our pleasure and profitts* . . . it is propounded unto us this day, wee shall surely perishe out of the good land whither we passe over this vast sea to possesse it." That profit should be called a false god follows inevitably from this very Calvinist ethic of radical openhandedness.

Another expression of this ethic is a sermon by Jonathan Edwards titled "Christian Charity; Or, The Duty of Charity to the Poor, Explained and Enforced." The title of this lecture comes from the text quoted and expounded on by Edwards, Deuteronomy 15:7–11, as it appears in the 1611 King James Version. "If there be among you a poor man of one of thy brethren within any of thy gates . . . thou shalt open thy hand wide unto him," and again, "Thou shalt open thine hand wide unto thy brother, to thy poor, and to thy needy, in thy land." The word *wide* does not occur in other translations. It is very much to Edwards's point, however, which is that the obligation to charity has no limits. Like Calvin and Winthrop he argues that "the general state and nature of mankind . . . renders it most reasonable that we should love our neighbors as ourselves; for men are made in the image of our God, and on this account are worthy of our love." The proper objects of our liberality are not limited to "those of the same people and religion" because "our enemies, those that abuse us and injure us, are our neighbours, and therefore come under the rule of loving our neighbors as ourselves." Like Calvin and Winthrop, Edwards states and answers every objection, or excuse, that would make generosity selective, from the limits of the giver's means to the unworthiness of the potential receiver, including finally the fact that the poor were provided relief by the town. Of this he says, "[I]t doth not answer the rules of christian charity, to relieve only those who are reduced to extremity," and "[I]t is too obvious to be denied, that there are in fact persons so in want, that it would be a charitable act in us to help them, notwithstanding all that is done by the town. A man must hide his mental eyes, to think otherwise."

At present, here in what is still sometimes called our Calvinist civilization, the controversies of liberalism and conservatism come down, as always, to economics. How exclusive is our claim to what we earn, own, inherit? Are the poor among us injured by the difficulties of their lives, or are the better among them braced and stimulated by the pinch of want? Is Edwards undermining morality when he says "it is better to give to several that are not objects of charity, than to send away empty one that is"? Would we be better friends of traditional values, therefore better Christians, if we exploited the coercive potential of need on the one hand and help on the other? There is clearly a feeling abroad that God smiled on our beginnings, and that we should return to them as we can. If we really did attempt to return to them, we would find Moses as well as Christ, Calvin, and his legions of intellectual heirs. And we would find a recurrent, passionate insistence on bounty or liberality, mercy and liberality, on being kind and liberal, liberal and bountiful, and enjoying the great blessings God has promised to liberality to the poor. These phrases are all Edwards's and there are many more like them.

Calvin says, in a sermon on Deuteronomy 15, "[A]s God bestoweth his benefites upon us, let us beware that wee acknowledge it towardes him, by doing good to our neighbors whome he offereth unto us, so as wee neither exempt ourselves from their want, nor seclude them from our abundance, but gently make them partakers with us, as folke that are linked togither in an inseparable bond."

From the depths of my heart, I say, Amen.

When I Was a Child

When I was a child I read books. My reading was not indiscriminate. I preferred books that were old and thick and hard. I made vocabulary lists.

Surprising as it may seem, I had friends, some of whom read more than I did. I knew a good deal about Constantinople and the Cromwell revolution and chivalry. There was little here that was relevant to my experience, but the shelves of northern Idaho groaned with just the sort of old dull books I craved, so I cannot have been alone in these enthusiasms.

Relevance was precisely not an issue for me. I looked to Galilee for meaning and to Spokane for orthodonture, and beyond that the world where I was I found entirely sufficient.

It may seem strange to begin a talk about the West in terms of old books that had nothing Western about them, and of naive fabrications of stodgily fantastical, authoritative worlds, which answered only to my own forming notions of meaning and importance. But I think it was in fact peculiarly Western to feel no tie of particularity to any single past or history, to experience that much underrated thing called deracination, the meditative, free appreciation of whatever comes under one's eye, without any need to make such tedious judgments as "mine" and "not mine."

I went to college in New England and I have lived in Massachusetts for twenty years, and I find that the hardest work in the world—it may in fact be impossible—is to persuade Eastern-ers that growing up in the West is not intellectually crippling. On learning that I am from Idaho, people have not infrequently asked, "Then how were you able to write a book?"

Once or twice, when I felt cynical or lazy, I have replied, "I went to Brown," thinking that might appease them—only to be asked, "How did you manage to get into Brown?" One woman, on learning of my origins, said, "But there *has* to be talent in the family *some*where."

In a way *Housekeeping* is meant as a sort of demonstration of the intellectual culture of my childhood. It was my intention to make only those allusions that would have been available to my narrator, Ruth, if she were me at her age, more or less. The classical allusions, Carthage sown with salt and the sowing of dragon's teeth which sprouted into armed men, stories that Ruthie combines, were both in the Latin textbook we used at Coeur d'Alene High School. My brother David brought home the fact that God is a sphere whose center is everywhere and whose circumference is nowhere. I never thought to ask him where he found it. Emily Dickinson and the Bible were bless-edly unavoidable.

There are not many references in *Housekeeping* to sources other than these few, though it is a very allusive book, because the narrator deploys every resource she has to try to make the world comprehensible. What she knows, she uses, as she does her eyes and her hands. She appropriates the ruin of Carthage for the purposes of her own speculation. I thought the lore my teachers urged on me must have some such use.

Idaho society at that time at least seemed to lack the sense of social class which elsewhere makes culture a system of signs and passwords, more or less entirely without meaning except as it identifies groups and subgroups. I think it is indifference to these codes among Westerners that makes Easterners think they are without culture. These are relative differences, of course,

and wherever accident grants a little reprieve from some human folly it must be assumed that time is running out and the
immunity is about to disappear.

As an aspect of my own intellectual life as a bookish child
in the far West I was given odds and ends—Dido pining on
her flaming couch, Lewis and Clark mapping the wilderness—
without one being set apart from the other as especially likely
to impress or satisfy anyone. We were simply given these things
with the assurance that they were valuable and important in
no specific way. I imagine a pearl diver finding a piece of statu-
ary under the Mediterranean, a figure immune to the crush of
depth though up to its waist in sand and blue with cold, in tat-
ters of seaweed, its eyes blank with astonishment, its lips parted
to make a sound in some lost dialect, its hand lifted to a city
long since lost beyond indifference.

The diver might feel pity at finding so human a thing in so
cold a place. It might be his privilege to react with a sharper
recognition than anyone in the living world could do, though
he had never heard the name of Phidias or Myron. The things
we learned were in the same way, merely given for us to make
what meaning we could of them.

This extended metaphor comes to you courtesy of Mrs.
Bloomsburg, my high-school Latin teacher, who led five or six
of us through Horace and Virgil and taught us patience with
that strange contraption called the epic simile, which, to compare
great things with small, appears fairly constantly in my own
prose, modified for my own purposes. It was also Mrs. Bloomsburg who trudged us through Cicero's vast sentences, clause depending from clause, the whole cantilevered with subjunctives
and weighted with a culminating irony. It was all over our heads.
We were bored but dogged. And at the end of it all, I think anyone can see that my style is considerably more indebted to Cicero than to Hemingway.

I admire Hemingway. It is simply an amusing accident

that it should be Cicero, of all people, whose influence I must resist. This befell me because I was educated at a certain time in a certain place. When I went to college in New England, I found that only I and a handful of boys prepared by Jesuits shared these quaint advantages. In giving them to Ruth I used her to record the intellectual culture of the West as I experienced it myself.

The peculiarities of my early education are one way in which being from the West has set me apart. A man in Alabama asked me how I felt the West was different from the East and the South, and I replied that in the West "lonesome" is a word with strongly positive connotations. I must have phrased my answer better at the time, because both he and I were struck by the aptness of the remark, and people in Alabama are far too sensitive to language to be pleased with a phrase such as "strongly positive connotations." For the moment it will have to serve, however.

I remember when I was a child at Coolin or Sagle or Talache, walking into the woods by myself and feeling the solitude around me build like electricity and pass through my body with a jolt that made my hair prickle. I remember kneeling by a creek that spilled and pooled among rocks and fallen trees with the unspeakably tender growth of small trees already sprouting from their backs, and thinking, there is only one thing wrong here, which is my own presence, and that is the slightest imaginable intrusion—feeling that my solitude, my loneliness, made me almost acceptable in so sacred a place.

I remember the evenings at my grandparents' ranch, at Sagle, and how in the daytime we chased the barn cats and swung on the front gate and set off pitchy, bruising avalanches in the woodshed, and watched my grandmother scatter chicken feed from an apron with huge pockets in it, suffering the fractious contentment of town children rusticated. And then the cows came home and the wind came up and Venus burned through what little remained of the atmosphere and the dark and the emptiness stood over the old house like some unsought revelation.

It must have been at evening that I heard the word "lonesome" spoken in tones that let me know the privilege attached to it, the kind of democratic privilege that comes with simple deserving. I think it is correct to regard the West as a moment in history much larger than its own. My grandparents and people like them had a picture in their houses of a stag on a cliff, admiring a radiant moon, or a maiden in classical draperies, on the same cliff, admiring the same moon. It was a specimen of decayed Victorianism. In that period mourning, melancholy, regret, and loneliness were high sentiments, as they were for the psalmist and for Sophocles, for the Anglo-Saxon poets and for Shakespeare.

In modern culture these are seen as pathologies—alienation and inauthenticity in Europe, maladjustment and depression in the United States. At present, they seem to flourish only in vernacular forms, country-and-western music being one of these. The moon has gone behind a cloud, and I'm so lonesome I could die.

It seems to me that, within limits the Victorians routinely transgressed, the exercise of finding the ingratiating qualities of grave or fearful experience is very wholesome and stabilizing. I am vehemently grateful that, by whatever means, I learned to assume that loneliness should be in part pleasure, sensitizing and clarifying, and that it is even a truer bond among people than any kind of proximity. It may be mere historical conditioning, but when I see a man or a woman alone, he or she looks mysterious to me, which is only to say that for a moment I see another human being clearly.

I am praising that famous individualism associated with Western and American myth. When I praise anything, I proceed from the assumption that the distinctions available to us in this world are not arrayed between good and bad but between bad and worse. Tightly knit communities in which members look to one another for identity, and to establish meaning and value, are disabled and often dangerous, however polished their veneer. The opposition frequently made between individualism on the one hand and responsibility to society on the other is a false opposition as we all know. Those who look at things from a little distance can never be valued sufficiently.

But arguments from utility will never produce true individualism. The cult of the individual is properly aesthetic and religious. The significance of every human destiny is absolute and equal. The transactions of conscience, doubt, acceptance, rebellion are privileged and unknowable. Insofar as such ideas are accessible to proof, I have proved the truth of this view to my entire satisfaction. Of course, they are not accessible to proof.

Only lonesomeness allows one to experience this sort of radical singularity, one's greatest dignity and privilege. Understanding this permits one to understand the sacred poetry in strangeness, silence, and otherness. The vernacular form of this idea is the Western hero, the man of whom nothing can ever really be known.

By this oblique route I have arrived at the question of the frontier, which, I would propose, was neither a place nor a thing, neither a time nor a historical condition. At the simplest level, it amounted to no more than the movement of European-origin people into a part of the world where they had no business being. By the mid-nineteenth century, this was very old news. The same thing had happened on every continent, save Antarctica.

In this context, it is best that I repeat my governing assumption, that history is a dialectic of bad and worse. The history of European civilization vis-à-vis the world from the fifteenth century to the present day is astounding and terrible. The worst aspects of settlement were by no means peculiar to the American West, but some of its better aspects may well have been. On the one hand, the settlement was largely done by self-selecting populations who envisaged permanent settlement on land that, as individuals or communally, they would own outright. The penal colonies and pauper colonies and slash-and-burn raids on the wealth of the land which made the history of the most colonized places so unbelievably desolate were less significant here. On the other, there was a Utopian impulse, the hope to create a model of a good human order, that seems to have arrived on the *Mayflower*, and which flourished through the whole of the nineteenth century. By the standards that apply to events of its kind, the Western settlement had a considerable positive content.

I have read fairly extensively over the last few years nineteenth-century writing about American social and political issues. Whether or not the West would be settled was clearly not in doubt. The question was how, and by whom. It appears to me that the Homestead Act was designed to consolidate the North's victory in the Civil War by establishing an economy of smallholder farming, of the kind that prevailed in the North, as opposed to plantation farming on the Southern model. English agriculture was very close to the kind practiced in the South, with the exception that the gangs of English farm laborers, though so poor they were usually called "wretches," were not technically slaves or chattel. In attempting to give the Western lands over to people in parcels suitable to making individual families the owners of the means of their subsistence— and the language I am using here is nineteenth-century and American—Lincoln contained, more or less, the virtual slavery that followed actual slavery. In terms of the time, as things go in this world, the policies that opened the West were sophisticated, considered, and benign. No wonder such hope was attached to them.

The American frontier was what it was because it expressed a considerable optimism about what people were and what they might become. Writers of the period assumed that human nature was deformed by drudgery, poverty, contempt, and self-contempt. They were obsessed with the fact that most people in most places—including American blacks on plantations and American whites in city slums—lived lives that were bitterly unworthy of them.

So it is not surprising that their heroes lived outside society, and neither did nor suffered the grueling injuries that were the stuff of ordinary life. In Whitman the outsider is a visionary. In Thoreau he is a critic. In the vernacular tradition of Western myth he is a rescuer and avenger. In every version he expresses discontent with society. So it is not surprising that he is the creation of generations that accomplished more radical reforms of society than had ever been attempted anywhere before.

This brings me around again to an earlier point, that there is no inevitable conflict between individualism as an ideal and a very positive interest in the good of society.

Obviously I have an ax to grind here. My one great objection to the American hero was that he was inevitably male—in decayed forms egregiously male. So I created a female hero, of sorts, also an outsider and a stranger. And while Sylvie obviously has her own history, to the degree that she has not taken the impress of society she expresses the fact that human nature is replete with nameless possibilities and, by implication, that the world is accessible to new ways of understanding.

Perhaps it was a misfortune for us that so many interesting ideas were associated with access to a habitable wilderness. The real frontier need never close. Everything, for all purposes, still remains to be done.

I think it is a universal sorrow that society, in every form in which it has ever existed, precludes and forecloses much that we find loveliest and most ingratiating in others and in ourselves. Rousseau said men are born free, yet everywhere they are in chains. Since the time of the Hebrew prophets it has been the role of the outsider to loosen these chains, or lengthen them, if only by bringing the rumor of a life lived otherwise.

That said, I must say too how beautiful human society seems to me, especially in those attenuated forms so characteristic of the West—isolated towns and single houses which sometimes offer only the merest, barest amenities: light, warmth, supper, familiarity. We have colonized a hostile planet, and we must stanch every opening where cold and dark might pour through and destroy the false climates we make, the tiny simulations of forgotten seasons beside the Euphrates, or in Eden. At a certain level housekeeping is a regime of small kindnesses, which, taken together, make the world salubrious, savory, and warm. I think of the acts of comfort offered and received within a household as precisely sacramental. It is the sad tendency of domesticity—as of piety—to contract and of grace to decay into rigor and peace into tedium. Still it should be clear why I find the Homestead Act all in all the most poetic piece of legislation since Deuteronomy, which it resembles.

Over years I have done an archaeology of my own thinking, mainly to attempt an escape from assumptions that would embarrass me if I understood their origins. In the course of this reeducation I have become suspiciously articulate and opinionated about things no doubt best left to the unself-conscious regions of the mind. At the same time, I feel I have found a place in the West for my West, and the legitimation of a lifelong intuition that the spirit of this place is, as spirits go, mysterious, aloof, and rapturously gentle. It is, historically, among other things, the orphan child of a brilliant century.

I think it is fair to say that the West has lost its place in the national imagination because, by some sad evolution, the idea of human nature has become the opposite of what it was when the myth of the West began, and now people who are less shaped and constrained by society are assumed to be disabled and dangerous. This is bad news for the American psyche, a fearful and antidemocratic idea, which threatens to close down change. I think it would be a positively good thing for the West to assert itself in the most interesting terms, so that the whole country must hear and be reanimated by dreams and passions it has too casually put aside and too readily forgotten.

The Fate of Ideas: Moses

There is an outpouring these days of scholarly-looking books about the Bible. They might appear to depart from more traditional works on this venerable subject in their tone of condescension toward biblical texts and narratives, toward the culture that produced them, toward God. But these books in fact continue, however unwittingly, a tradition which is both long and unsavory.

We are culturally predisposed to sheltering criticism from criticism; we have enshrined the iconoclast. If our feelings register some minor shock, or if we suppose the public might be somewhat irked, or even if we think we can discern some earnest hope on the part of a writer to irk or to offend ourselves or our neighbors, then a book is praised as a creditable effort and excused from the kind of attention that might raise questions about its actual novelty or merit.

The intention behind these books seems to be only the one that is usual just now, to discredit in the course of laying blame. This is the purpose and method of much contemporary scholarship. Debunking exhausts its subjects, which must have some remnant of respectability about them to give meaning, or at least frisson, to the enterprise. And since the Bible does have a certain aura of sanctity about it yet, it offers the hope that there is discrediting still to be done, and this makes it an attractive subject. The value of this critical project in general is not a question of great importance. But as a method of approach to the Bible it draws attention to issues that are of a high order of significance by reproducing in exaggerated forms attitudes that have affected the reading of these texts for centuries.

These grave and interesting problems arise because of the special history of the Bible and because of the polemics that have always surrounded it. More specifically, they arise from the complex and uneasy relation of the Old to the New Testament. This is an important aspect of the problem of Christian attitudes toward Judaism. (I will speak of the Old Testament rather than the Hebrew Bible because they have very different cultural histories, the order of the books is different, Hebrew and Aramaic hover around the latter in any form whereas Latin and vernacular translations have very much conditioned the reading of the former, and so on.) It has been orthodox through most of Christian history to treat the Old Testament as rigid, benighted, greatly inferior to the Gospels. This error has never been truly rectified. The Old Testament is very difficult to read, and the churches seem to do little in the way of making its hard texts accessible, so it is known largely by reputation, and its reputation is daunting. It is generally thought of as a tribal epic which includes the compendium of strange laws and fierce prohibitions Jesus of Nazareth put aside when he established the dominion of grace.

Since its prophets and poets can be read for texts that seem to promise the Christian Messiah, and since the Gospels and Epistles allude freely to Adam and Moses and Abraham, the significance of the Old Testament cannot be denied. And yet Christianity has tended to define itself by implied or direct disparagement of the Old Testament. The unloveliness of appropriating the sacred literature of another religion in order to put it to such use is hard to overstate. Worse, where Christianity itself has been rejected, very frequently it is the Old Testament which bears the brunt of disparagement, Jesus being allowed to escape on grounds of pathos and harmlessness. These lamentable habits are visibly at work in most of these new books. The historical consequences of such thinking forbid that impressive evidence of its continuing vigor should go unremarked.

The Episcopal bishop John Shelby Spong published a book called *Why Christianity Must Change or Die* (1998). It is a commonplace among churchmen that great institutional and doctrinal change is needed urgently to bring the faith abreast of changes that have already occurred in the culture. Bishop Spong is perhaps more forthright than others, arguing for the shelving of the Ten Commandments on the grounds that "this supposedly divine code has been abandoned wherever it has become inconvenient." For example, in the matter of graven images, "our churches are filled with them, from crosses to crucifixes to tabernacles to ambreys to icons to stations of the cross. So the commandment against graven images has become irrelevant." This is an example of the curious insularity of his thinking. A great many churches are empty of all these things, with or without the exception of crosses, in deference to that very commandment. And there are, need I say, temples and synagogues where it is still observed most scrupulously.

Perhaps the sanctity of divine law does indeed rest on its aligning itself with Episcopalian practice. We will all find out when the trumpet sounds. In the meantime, a question we *can* usefully address is raised by terms in which the bishop dismisses the Ten Commandments and the Torah, that is, the first five books of the Old Testament. He says, "This mythology of a divine source of ethics enforced by the all-seeing God . . . has been revealed by the ancient codes themselves to be utter nonsense. A careful study of these codes reveals nothing less [he probably means "nothing more"] than the tribal prejudices, stereotypes, and limited knowledge of the people who created them. That is certainly true of the Torah and even more of the

Ten Commandments." This would appear to any dispassionate reader as blatant and illiberal disrespect for another religion, if it were not true of these most cherished Hebrew
scriptures that we Christians stole them fair and square, acquiring even the right—perhaps the obligation!—to regard
them with contempt. Surely I am not alone in feeling there is
something very wrong here.

In fairness, Christianity also suffers terribly at the hands
of Bishop Spong, though he may not be wholly conscious of
this fact. He gives an account, with Episcopal self-assurance,
of what Christians believe, which I, who have long answered
to that description, read with true astonishment. According to
him, our assumptions about God are based on the notion of a
three-tier universe: heaven above, hell below, and between
them a flat earth. God, enthroned in heaven, can look down on
us all and keep track of what we do. This derives, supposedly,
from the Old Testament. But the earth, the bishop tells us, has
been proved by science to be spherical! And space to be empty!
He is heroic in his pursuit of the implications of this myth-
shattering roundness so lately recognized as a feature of our
planet. He explains that it makes nonsense of Christ's ascen-
sion: "When citizens of China and the United States point upward, they are pointing in diametrically opposite directions.
'Up' is a spatial image. It reflects the assumption that the flat
earth is the center of the universe, and, as such, it is incomprehensible to the modern mind." It's amazing we post-Copernicans
can even get out of bed. But, Bishop Spong continues, "Today, if
one could rise from this earth in an upward trajectory [the best
sort of trajectory, if one is to rise at all] and go far enough, that
person would not arrive in heaven but would rather achieve an
orbit or, by escaping the gravitational pull of earth, would jour-
ney into the infinite depths of space." I feel I must appeal here
to the kindness of my non- and post-Christian readers. Regard-

ing all such supposed issues of faith, believe me, to the best of my knowledge the bishop speaks for himself.

Something of serious importance is transacted in this book, however. Bishop Spong rescues Jesus not only from the conceptual archaism he feels distorts the meaning of the New Testament and the Creeds but also, very disturbingly, from the moral and ethical primitivity which he finds in the Old Testament. Spong's God is the Ground of Being, and his Jesus a realization of life, love, and wholeness, who calls us "to be all that we can be." Finally Christianity can put down its cross. For, as the bishop notes—and who will dispute it?—"a human father who would nail his son to a cross for any purpose would be arrested for child abuse." Why do I feel compelled to note that Jesus was thirty-three?

It is entirely appropriate for Christians to come to whatever terms they must with the difficulties of their own sacred narrative, their own mythopoesis. But the Old Testament is another matter. It is not in the same sense theirs, and if they refuse to grant it its terms, or to give it their respectful attention, then it is not theirs in any sense at all. When Bishop Spong says, "The Jewish God in the Hebrew scriptures was assumed to hate anyone that the nation of Israel hated," he offers no evidence of the truth of his harshly negative remark. The assumption is made that Israel and "the Jewish God" are both given to hatred, when two great exemplary figures of righteousness and graciousness in the Old Testament, Job and Ruth, are not Jews, are in fact an Edomite and a Moabite, despised people if one were to believe what one is told about the narrow tribalism of the Hebrew scriptures. Jonah is sent to save terrifying Nineveh, a great enemy city, which "the Jewish God" cares for and is at pains to spare. However one passage or another might be read, there is much unambiguous evidence of striking universalism to discredit this hostile characterization of the Hebrew scriptures. Elsewhere the bishop says that Jesus "lived in a world where cultural barriers were drawn that defined women as subhuman and children as not worthy of God's concern." He offers no evidence of the truth of this statement, and, coincidentally perhaps, the Bible contains no evidence of the truth of it.

If what is desired is a God who presents no difficulties and makes no demands, the Old Testament must surely be rejected. But to reject it is one thing, to denounce it is another, and to misrepresent it in the course of denouncing it is another still. The Old Testament is not for Christians to denounce because we need only put it respectfully aside, as a Methodist might the Book of Mormon, as a Jew might the New Testament. The Old Testament certainly is not ours to misrepresent, since in doing so we slander the culture we took it from, an old and very evil habit among us. Since Friedrich Nietzsche seems to be on every curriculum, unshakably canonized for all his deadness, whiteness, and maleness, I need only mention his familiar theory that Judeo-Christianity was foisted on Europeans by vengeful Jews. I have never seen anyone else even speculate as to how it has come about that we consider ourselves victimized for having made inappropriate use of someone else's scriptures. Yet this sense of victimization is everywhere—it is even proposed in certain of these books that the Old Testament predisposed us to genocide.

After centuries of neglect and suppression the Old Testament became a much studied and lovingly translated text at the time of the Reformation. Its beauty rewarded the attention of Christian humanists and was the occasion for the definitive emergence of modern languages such as English and German as literary languages. The religious significance ascribed to it and the method by which it was interpreted varied with the theological setting in which it found itself. Yet never was it justly dealt with or properly valued by any major Christian tradition, nor is it now.

In his *Utopia*, Thomas More, the sixteenth-century statesman and scholar, notes one great difference between the regime of Christian England and the laws laid down by Moses. English thieves were hanged in great numbers, sometimes twenty on a scaffold, whereas "to be short, Moses' law, though it were ungentle and sharp, as a law that was given to bondmen, yea, and them very obstinate, stubborn and stiff-necked, *yet it punished theft by the purse, and not with death* [emphasis mine]. And let us not think that God in the new law of clemency and mercy, under the which He ruleth us with fatherly gentleness, as his dear children, hath given us greater scope and license to the execution of cruelty upon one another." More wrote his book in Latin, and the learned could not be hanged (if they were male)— this is the actual meaning of the phrase "benefit of clergy"—so those to whom his thoughts would have been of pressing interest would not have been among his readers. But a very valuable point is made here, which is seldom made, and which, if we were honest, would force us to consider many things.

Moses (by whom I mean the ethos and spirit of Mosaic law, however it came to be articulated) in fact does not authorize any physical punishment for crimes against property. The entire economic and social history of Christendom would have been transformed if Moses had been harkened to only in this one particular. Feudalism, not to mention early capitalism, is hardly to be imagined where such restraint was observed in defense of the rights of ownership. Anyone familiar with European history is aware of the zeal for brutal punishment, the terrible ingenuity with which the human body was tormented and insulted through the eighteenth century at least, very often to deter theft on the part of the wretched. Moses authorizes nothing of the kind, nor indeed does he countenance any oppression of the poor. More is entirely conventional, as he would be still, in describing the law of Moses as "sharp" beside the merciful governance of Christ. But how could Europe have been more effectively Christianized—understand the sense in which I use the word—than by adherence to these laws of Moses? Granting the severity of the holiness codes in the Torah, they do not compare unfavorably with laws touching religious matters in More's England. More himself called for the burning of William Tyndale, the great early translator of the Bible into English, who was in fact burned. It is often said that Europeans learned religious intolerance from the Old Testament. Then how did we happen to skip over the parts where the laws protect and provide for the poor, and where oppression of them is most fiercely forbidden? It is surely dishonest to suggest we learned anything at all from the Torah, if we have not learned anything good from it. Better to say our vices are our own than to try to exculpate ourselves by implying that our attention strayed during the humane and visionary passages. The law of Moses puts liberation theology to shame in its passionate loyalty to the poor. Why do we not know this yet?

Utopia describes the consequences of the nightmarish policy of clearance and enclosure, persisted in for centuries, which drove the rural poor out of the English countryside:

> For look in what parts of the realm doth grow the finest and therefore dearest wool, there noblemen and gentlemen, yea and certain abbots, holy men no doubt . . . much annoying the pubic weal, leave no room for tillage. They enclose all into pastures; they throw down houses; they pluck down towns, and leave nothing standing but a church to be made a sheep-house . . . [The poor] must needs depart away, poor, silly, wretched souls, men, women, husbands, wives, fatherless children, widows, woeful mothers with their young babes . . . Away they

trudge, I say, out of their known and accustomed houses, finding no place to rest in . . . [When they have sold whatever they have] what can they else to do but steal, and then justly be hanged, or else go about a-begging? And yet then also they be cast in prison as vagabonds, because they go out and work not, whom no man will set a-work, though they never so willingly proffer themselves thereto.

As I will demonstrate from the text, all this violates the laws of Moses, in letter and in spirit. How it is to be reconciled with any conceivable intention of Jesus I cannot imagine, but that is not the issue here. In fact, the laws of Moses establish a highly coherent system for minimizing and alleviating poverty, a brilliant economics based in a religious ethic marked by nothing more strongly than by an anxious solicitude for the well-being of the needy and the vulnerable.

Ah, but the people Moses brought out of slavery invaded and took the land of the Canaanites! The Israelites are much abused these days for their treatment of the Canaanites. The historicity of the invasion stories as they occur in Joshua is questionable; archaeology does not confirm them. Nor does the book of Judges, which names the peoples "the Lord left" in Canaan: Philistines, Sidonians, Hivites, Hittites, Amorites, Perizzites, and Jebusites (Judges 3:3–5). The Israelites may well have been Canaanites themselves, or a mixed population of those who were slaves in Egypt rather than a tribe or people. The number of those who left Egypt may have been small and have grown in retrospect, like the French Resistance. Possession of Canaan was never complete. Other inhabitants, for example Hittites and Philistines, were also invaders. Ancient Near Eastern records often describe the defeat of enemies as their extermination; in fact the one known mention of Israel in Egyptian writing, dated about 1230 BCE, boasts that "Israel is laid waste, his seed is not."

In any case, whatever happened in Canaan, a violent epic was made of it which is the basis for much vilification of "the Jewish God."

As ancient narrative, and as history, this story of conquest is certainly the least remarkable part of the Bible, and a very modest event as conquests go, the gradual claiming of an enclave in a territory that would be utterly negligible by the lights of real conquerors such as Alexander the Great or Augustus Caesar or even Ashurbanipal. The suggestion that God was behind it maybe makes it worse than the campaigns of self-aggrandizement that destroyed many larger and greater cities, though it is not clear to me that it should. A consequence which follows from God's role in the conquest of Canaan, asserted with terrible emphasis in Leviticus and elsewhere, is that God will deal with the Israelites exactly as he has dealt with the Canaanites, casting them out of the land in their turn if they cease to deserve it. Abraham is told in a dream that possession of the promised land will be delayed an astonishing four hundred years until, in effect, the Amorites (that is, Canaanites) have lost their right to it. We Anglo-European invaders do not know yet if we will have four hundred years in *this* land.

Furthermore, as they approach Canaan, the Hebrews are told that they may not take any land of the Edomites or the Moabites because God has already given those people their lands, having driven out former inhabitants (Deuteronomy 2:4–11). This is not the thinking of racial supremacists, or of people who believe they alone have God's attention. Certainly it implies that God honors righteousness in those outside the Abrahamic covenant—otherwise the Canaanites could not have held the land while they did. In any case, only ignorance can excuse the notion that Europeans learned aggression and tribalism while perusing the Bible. The Peloponnesian Wars by themselves are a sufficient demonstration of this point.

•

Assuming that my readers are, for the most part, nonindige-
nous as I am, I would like to raise the question that seems to
me as relevant to ourselves as to Moses. The movements of
populations, that great mysterious fact, are always full of disruption and grief and regret and are as inevitable and irreversible as the drift of continents. Say that my ancestors fled poverty
or affliction elsewhere, as the old Hebrews did, and caused
poverty and dispossession here. Granting that they were invaders, they might still have drawn conclusions from hard experience about how society could be made just, which were
generous and a laudable conversion of bitterness into hope.
The most beautiful laws of Moses, when they are noticed at
all, are as if shamed and discredited by the fact that he brought
his tired and poor to settle in a land that was already populated. We have learned to think of our own most beautiful laws
in the same way. Are disruption and dispossession somehow
redeemed by contempt for their best consequences? Clearly, it
was the inspiration of Moses to exploit what might be called
the culturelessness of people who had lived for centuries as
outsiders in tradition-bound Egypt, in order to make a new
nation with a distinctive religious culture which would express
itself in a new social order. In the narrative, his laws are for-
mulated before the entry into Canaan, implying that the vision of the society preexisted the society itself—and, indeed,
was like a prophetic vision, always still to be realized. If the
purpose of the law is the righteousness of the individual, its purpose is also the goodness of individual and communal life. If
each member of the community obeys the commandments, then
all members receive the assurance that they will not be murdered, that their households will not be robbed or disrupted,
that they will not be slandered, that their children will not

abuse or abandon them. The relation of law to prophecy, of prohibition to liberation, is very clear.

The laws of Moses assume that the land is God's, that the Hebrews are strangers and sojourners there who cannot really own it but who enjoy it at God's pleasure (Leviticus 25:23). The land is apportioned to the tribes, excepting the priestly Levites. It can be sold (the assumption seems to be that this would be done under pressure of debt or poverty) but a kinsman has the right to buy it back, that is, redeem it, and restore it to its owner. In any case, in every fiftieth year the lands are restored to the tribes and households to whom they were first given. Every seventh year Hebrew slaves are freed, each taking with him or her enough of the master's goods to "furnish him liberally" (Deuteronomy 15:14; all quotations are from the Revised Standard Version). In these years also all debts are to be forgiven. Obviously these laws would have the effect of preventing accumulation of wealth and preventing as well the emergence of a caste of people who are permanently dispossessed. Furthermore, in every seventh year the *land* is to have a Sabbath, to lie fallow, "that the poor of your people may eat; and what they leave the wild beasts may eat" (Exodus 23:11). Others are to live on what it produces without cultivation and on what has been set aside (Leviticus 25:1–7, 20–23). At all times people are forbidden to reap the corners of their fields, to glean after they have reaped, to harvest their vineyards and their olive trees thoroughly, to go back into the field for a sheaf they have forgotten: "It shall be for the sojourner, the fatherless, and the widow. You shall remember that you were a slave in the land of Egypt; therefore I command you to do this" (Deuteronomy 24:21–22).

These laws would preserve those who were poor from the kind of wretchedness More describes by giving them an assured subsistence. While charity in Christendom was urged as a virtue—one that has always been unevenly aspired to—here the poor have their portion at the hand of God, and at the behest of the law. If a commandment is something in the nature of a promise ("Ten Commandments" is an English imposition; in Hebrew they are called the Ten Words), then not only "you will not be stolen from" but also "you will not steal" would be in some part fulfilled, first because the poor are given the right to take what would elsewhere have been someone else's property, and second because they are sheltered from the extreme of desperation that drives the needy to theft. The law of Moses so far values life above property that it forbids killing a thief who is breaking and entering by daylight (Exodus 22:2). Judgment in criminal matters is based on the testimony of at least two witnesses, and not, as in premodern European civil law, on judicial torture and self-incrimination, which often led to the deaths of accused who insisted on their innocence. In very many ways Moses would have lifted a terrible onus of manslaughter from the whole civilization. The benefits to everyone involved in terms of dignity and peace would have been incalculable.

And it is certainly to be noted that no conditions limit God's largesse toward the poor. They need not be pious, or Jewish, or worthy, or conspicuously in need, or intent on removing themselves from their condition of dependency. The Bible never considers the poor otherwise than with tender respect, and this is fully as true when the speaker is "the Jewish God" as it is when the speaker is Jesus. What laws could be more full of compassion than these?

> You shall not oppress a stranger; you know the heart
> of a stranger, for you were strangers in the land of
> Egypt.   Exodus 23:9

> You shall not give up to his master a slave who has escaped from his master to you; he shall dwell with you,

in your midst, in the place which he shall choose within one of your towns, where it pleases him best; you shall not oppress him.   Deuteronomy 23:15–16

You shall not pervert the justice due to the sojourner or to the fatherless, or take a widow's garment in pledge.
                                        Deuteronomy 24:17

You shall not oppress a hired servant who is poor and needy, whether he is one of your brethren or one of the sojourners who are in your land within your towns; you shall give him his hire on the day he earns it, before the sun goes down (for he is poor, and sets his heart upon it); lest he cry against you to the Lord, and it be sin in you.
                                        Deuteronomy 25:14–15

If there is among you a poor man, one of your brethren, in any of your towns within your land which the Lord your God gives you, you shall not harden your heart or shut your hand against your poor brother, but you shall open your hand to him, and lend him sufficient for his need, whatever it may be . . . You shall give to him freely, and your heart shall not be grudging when you give to him; because for this the Lord your God will bless you in all your work and all that you undertake. For the poor will never cease out of the land; therefore I command you, You shall open wide your hand to your brother, to the needy and to the poor, in the land.   Deuteronomy 15:7–8, 10–11

Then there is a Sabbath, the day in which one may not exploit and cannot be exploited, even by one's family or oneself.

Six days you shall labor and do all your work; but the seventh day is a sabbath to the Lord your God; in it you shall not do any work, you, or your son, or your daughter, or your manservant, or your maidservant, or your ox, or your ass, or any of your cattle, or the sojourner who is within your gates, that your manservant and your maidservant may rest as well as you. You shall remember that you were a servant in the land of Egypt, and the Lord your God brought you out thence with a mighty hand and an outstretched arm; therefore the Lord your God commanded you to keep the sabbath day. Deuteronomy 5:12–15

Exhaustion was as endemic as malnutrition among the laboring classes of European cultures into the twentieth century. Moses obliged manservant and maidservant, stranger and sojourner, ox and ass, to share in God's rest one day in seven. This is profoundly humane, quite unexampled. Some Christian writers on the Sabbath say this law has never applied to us, though historically many Christians have in fact sabbatized earnestly, one day late. Jesus, in the manner of a Jewish prophet, criticized the way in which the Sabbath was observed in his time, clearly feeling that it had become more demanding than restorative. This is far from a rejection of the institution itself, nor is it to be imagined that Jesus could have wished to deprive servants of their rest any more than widows and orphans and strangers of their sustenance. Yet all this has been done in his name because he supposedly freed us from the burden of the law. It seems to me fair to say that the loss of Moses was the defeat of Jesus, insofar as it was the hope of Jesus to bless and relieve the poor.

These are the laws of a passionate God. "Impassioned" is usually used by the Jewish Publication Society to translate the word other English translations render as "jealous." The

Hebrew stem apparently means "to grow red." "Jealous" comes from the same Greek root as "zealous," and the Greek words that derive from it are usually translated in the New Testament as "zeal" or "zealous." In its earliest English uses, for example in John Wycliffe's fourteenth-century translation of the Old Testament, "jealous" often has that meaning, suggesting ardor and devotion. In modern translations the Hebrew word is usually translated as "zeal" when the subject is a human being (as in 1 Kings 19:10), which must indicate an awareness of the wider meaning of the word. But "jealousy" is virtually always imputed to God. Jealousy has evolved into a very simple and unattractive emotion, in our understanding of it, and God is much abused for the fact of his association with it. Since translations are forever being laundered to remove complexity and loveliness, and since tradition is not a legitimate plea in these matters, one cannot help wondering how this particular archaism manages to survive untouched.

Scholarly books on the Scriptures typically claim objectivity and may sometimes aspire to it, though their definitions of objectivity inevitably vary with the intentions of their writers. But to assume a posture of seeming objectivity relative to any controverted subject is a very old polemical maneuver. David Hume, in an endnote to his *Natural History of Religion* (written in 1751, published in 1779), quotes Chevalier Ramsay, who quotes an imagined Chinese or Indian philosopher's reaction to Christianity: "The God of the Jews is a most cruel, unjust, partial, and fantastical being ... This chosen nation was ... the most stupid, ungrateful, rebellious and perfidious of all nations ... [God's son dies to appease his vindictive wrath, but the vast majority of the world are excluded from any benefit. This makes God] ... a cruel, vindictive tyrant, an impotent or a wrathful daemon." And so on.

Even pious critics seem never to remember that, in the Old Testament, the Jews were talking among themselves, interpreting their own experience to themselves. Every negative thing we know about them, every phrase that is used to condemn them, *they* supplied, in their incredible self-scrutiny and self-judgment. Who but the ancient Jews would have thought to blame themselves for, in effect, lying along the invasion route of the Babylonians? They preserved and magnified their vision of the high holiness of God by absorbing into themselves responsibility for their sufferings, and this made them passionately self-accusatory, in ways no other people would have thought of being. This incomparable literature would surely have been lost if they had imagined the use it would be put to, and had written to justify themselves and to defend their descendants in the eyes of the nations rather than to ponder their life in openness toward God. By what standard but their own could Israel have been considered ungrateful or rebellious or corrupt? Granting crimes and errors, which they recorded, and preserved and pondered the records of for centuries, and which were otherwise so historically minor that no one would ever have heard of them—how do these crimes compare with those of other peoples, their contemporaries or ours? When Hume wrote, the English gibbets More describes were still as full as ever. The grandeur of the Old Testament, and the fact that such great significance is attached to it, distracts readers from a sense of its unique communal inwardness. It is an endless reconciliation achieved at great cost by a people whose relation to God is astonishingly brave and generous. To misappropriate it as a damning witness against the Jews and "the Jewish God" is vulgar beyond belief. And not at all uncommon, therefore. It is useful to consider how the New Testament would read, if it had gone on to chronicle the Crusades and the Inquisition.

·

Recent treatments of the Bible consistently ignore the unambiguously humane aspects of the Old Testament, continuing ancient practice. Jack Miles, in his *God: A Biography* (1995), says, "Though the law codes of the Pentateuch make moderate provision for widows, orphans, foreigners, slaves, and others in vulnerable categories, provision is not required because of any special relation that the Lord has with such people." The passages quoted above encourage another view of the matter. There is no standard, ancient or modern, by which these cycles of release from debt and bondage—which are called "sabbaths" and which are meant to structure the life of the community— could be called "moderate provision." But the assumptions from which Miles proceeds preclude the discovery of benevolence in God. Miles makes God an amalgam of Ancient Near Eastern gods: "The equation is creator (*yahweh/elohim*) + cosmic destroyer (*Tiamat*) + warrior (*Baal*) = GOD, the composite protagonist of the Tanakh," the Tanakh being the Hebrew Bible. We do not have the makings of loving-kindness here. Miles does not capitalize the divine name because Hebrew does not capitalize. So it seems we are to assume Akkadian does.

Miles's book is a very good illustration of the interpretive consequences of the use of scholarship and its like. Tiamat is the Babylonian goddess of the sea and mother of the gods, who in fact attempts to prevent the destruction of her offspring, though she is finally provoked to cosmic war with Marduk. And Canaanitish Baal seems to have been a god of rain and fertility, not of war. The invoking of such lore looks scholarly, but it is long out-of-date, even if it were not otherwise questionable. There is simply no evidence to support the idea that God had any such origins. Miles acknowledges this in a long endnote. This dumbed-down pseudo-syncretism, which is put forward as an explanation of the complexity, the Godlikeness, of God in the Tanakh, contains implicitly the statement that the ancient Jews had no primary conception of the nature of the holy, and the statement that the core qualities of God are simply those which distinguished Baal and Tiamat—in Miles's view, at least. I invite the reader to consider the consequences for Miles's thesis if he had made God an amalgam of Baal and Tiamat, therefore of fertility and the sea, or motherhood. The attributes Miles discovers in God are Miles's assumptions about him projected onto his supposed progenitors. It looks like objectivity to place God in the landscape of Ancient Near Eastern religion and regard the narratives in which he figures as if they were the mythos of any other ancient cult. But if the reader of such evidence about that landscape as exists is tendentious, nothing could be less objective. This has been the curse of this style of biblical scholarship since the eighteenth century.

God: A Biography is not, and does not claim to be, literary or scholarly or theological. It reads the Hebrew Bible as if it were a Christian Bible, that is, as if it were ordered chronologically in terms of narrative, which it is not. It proceeds as if the books of the Tanakh were written in the order in which they are arranged, which they were not. Miles allows himself conclusions that are only available to him because of the arbitrariness of his approach. Whatever the point of the exercise, certainly no new insight is achieved. His "God of the Tanakh" is petulant and violent and thick, familiar enough, the God of the disparaged Testament.

Moses the Egyptian: The Memory of Egypt in Western Monotheism (1997) is the work of Jan Assmann, a major German Egyptologist. It dusts off Freud's old theory that Moses was in fact Egyptian. Therefore Moses would have been influenced, Assmann argues, by the monotheistic cult of Aton, which worshipped the solar disk. (More precisely, it seems the pharaoh worshipped Aton, and everyone else worshipped the pharaoh.) Aton tended to go down at night, and there are lovely hymns of relief at his rising in the morning—facts which suggest that this was a lesser order of monotheism, and that Moses's achievement is undiminished. This is another example of the tendentious use of scholarship. Assmann argues that the monotheism of Akhenaton, the pharaoh who founded the cult, was intolerant and hated, and its effects lingered to infect the monotheism of Moses, which was therefore also profoundly intolerant and hated. Obviously there is nothing inevitable here.

Assmann's argument is the sort of razzle-dazzle that depends on coinages like "mnemohistory," which is the exalted and useful discipline of interpreting history that collective memory has displaced and suppressed so thoroughly only the writer has an inkling even of the fact of suppression. In this cognitive implosion a fusion occurs between Moses and the Aton cultus which conventional history simply cannot achieve. Assmann is writing this book in response to Freud's abysmal question about the origins of anti-Semitism. "Strikingly enough, his [Freud's] question was not how the Gentiles, or the Christians, or the Germans came to hate the Jews, but 'how the Jew had become what he is and why he has attracted this undying hatred.'" He paraphrases Freud's answer thus: "Not the Jew but monotheism had attracted this undying hatred. By making Moses an Egyptian, [Freud] deemed himself able to shift the sources of negativity and intolerance out of Judaism and back to Egypt, and to show that the defining fundamentals of Jewish monotheism and mentality came from outside it." So we are to concede, apparently, that these *are* "the defining fundamentals of Jewish monotheism and mentality." Comment is unnecessary, though I will draw attention here to the notion of victimization I remarked on earlier. We Gentiles have the Torah to blame for our worst moments, it would appear.

Like others of these writers, Assmann argues that ancient polytheism was essentially tolerant, "cosmotheism," and readily accepted other gods, translating them into the terms of the culture that received them. Granting that Melqart, a god of Carthage, did indeed lounge around in a lion skin looking just like Hercules, we have the fact that Rome loathed Carthage and was despised in turn, and reduced that great city to bare earth. Athens and Sparta had just the same pantheon, and they fought to the death. And Rome conquered Greece, whose gods it had thoroughly Latinized. That is to say, whatever the merits of polytheism, at best it only obliged people to find other than religious grounds for hostility, which they were clearly very able to do. How the wars of the Hebrews against the Canaanites are more culpable than the wars of the Romans against the Etruscans I fail to see, or why anyone should imagine that these wars were less formative for European civilization than those distant, inconclusive wars among the Semites. Or, for that matter, why they do not prove that the character of the civilization was already formed when Rome set about the conquest of Italy. Miles attributes the structure of Western consciousness to monotheism on the grounds that "the Bible was the popular encyclopedia of the Middle Ages." But in fact through most of the Common Era in Europe the Bible, and especially the Old Testament, existed almost exclusively in Latin, a language incomprehensible to the great majority of people, who were in any case illiterate. So its influence is easily overstated. Yet ferocious intolerance has characterized most of Western history in the Common Era.

Polytheism is as fashionable now as it has been since fascism was in its prime. As a corollary to the current tendency to blame monotheism for intolerance and aggression and genocide, there is an assumption that polytheism must have been tolerant, pacific, and humane. This notion is old, too. In *The Natural History of Religion*, Hume says, "by limiting the powers and functions of its deities, [idolatry] naturally admits the gods of other sects and nations to a share of divinity, and renders all the various deities, as well as rites, ceremonies, or traditions, compatible with each other . . . [By comparison] when one sole ob-

ject of devotion is acknowledged, the worship of other deities
is regarded as absurd and impious."

It is striking to see how the cultural discourse is circling
on itself. Perhaps the real familiarity of their arguments explains why these writers I have looked at offer so little in the way
of evidence. For example, Assmann, the most scholarly of them,
says the Old Testament is deeply informed by aversion to
Egypt, then offers no support from the text. And, coincidentally perhaps, little evidence is to be found in the text. One
Mosaic law of unambiguous relevance, which goes unmen-
tioned by him, is Deuteronomy 23:7: "You shall not abhor an
Edomite, for he is your brother; you shall not abhor an Egyptian, because you were a sojourner in his land." This law provides that both Edomites and Egyptians may enter the assembly
of the Lord on favorable terms—after three generations that is,
which seems long, but which is liberal by comparison with the
ancient Athenians, for instance, who never naturalized the descendants of foreigners. Nor, as I understand, do the modern
Germans. This one verse is sufficient to demonstrate that there
was not hatred but in fact a certain bond between Hebrews and
Egyptians.

The idea that the hatred of the Other is the signal preoccupation of the Old Testament is carried to great lengths by
Regina Schwartz in *The Curse of Cain: The Violent Legacy of Monotheism* (1997). The following passage gives a fair sense of the
book:

> Western culture is laced throughout with a variety of
> institutions, marriage laws, laws concerning the rights
> of so-called minors, sodomy laws, and a less overt but
> equally insidious bourgeois morality that specifies
> which sexual practices and partners are permissible as
> strictly as Leviticus. These institutions that reduce
> women to property—wives owned by their husbands,

daughters owned by their fathers—are stubborn institutions that are the heirs of monotheistic thinking
about scarcity that have kept misogyny alive and well
long after the biblical period, institutions that regard
a sullied property—a land shared by a foreigner, an
adulterous woman—and other variations of multiple
allegiances (multiple gods, if you will), as anathema.
The tentacles of the injunction "you shall have no other
gods before me" reach throughout our social formations,
structuring identity as a delimited possession with a remarkable grip.

If there are Eastern or polytheistic cultures which cannot
be described in the same terms, or in much harsher terms,
Schwartz does not name them. So we must take her word for it
that monotheism has created misogyny and xenophobia and
all the rest in Western culture. For her, monotheism functions
as original sin has done traditionally. It is the ultimate source
of every evil. And it is entirely located in the Old Testament—
the New Testament is mentioned once, in a note. This is an
extraordinary burden of opprobrium to place on a literature that
was of distinctly secondary significance during the formative
stages of Western civilization, beside civil law and canon law
and common law and natural law, beside the New Testament
and the teachings of the Church, beside the customs and prejudices that survived Christianization. I think it unlikely that the
Norse or the Franks turned misogynist under the influence of
Moses. For some reason the grim prehistory of Christian Europe seems to deserve not a glance. Considering the view Christendom has taken of Mosaic law, there is no great reason to
imagine that its princelings were deep students of Leviticus.
Schwartz draws attention to the striking perdurability of
attitudes and approaches to biblical scholarship that arose in the
late eighteenth and early nineteenth centuries. This scholarship

was the work of Germans for the most part and it was profoundly influenced by emerging nationalism and anti-Semitism—and often brilliant, like so much that was done in Europe in those years. Schwartz draws attention to some highly questionable assumptions that survive and flourish in biblical criticism on the strength of that old prestige. Source criticism, which has given us J, E, P, D, and other such artifacts of learned speculation, was pioneered by Julius Wellhausen in the middle of the nineteenth century. This analytical method is so perfectly suited to conforming the text to the critic's assumptions about it that it establishes nothing. Yet it has profoundly conditioned the reading of the Bible, which is now assumed by many to have been patched and botched and redacted until its intelligibility is at best merely apparent. It is refreshing to see attention drawn to the extremely tenuous nature of so much of the seeming learnedness that cumbers writing about the Bible. Bishop Spong tells us in what order and for what reason the books of the New Testament were composed. Not surprisingly, his hypothesis—which is all in the world it is or can be—makes his interpretation of these texts seem downright inevitable. To offer hypothesis as fact is not fair to the nonspecialist readership for which his book is clearly intended. In doing so he is typical rather than exceptional among popular writers.

On the other hand, Schwartz's own approach is full of the mannerisms of contemporary scholarship, eager to indict, indifferent to the strengths and pleasures of the text. It is perhaps this approach which makes her insensitive in her own book to the worst tendency of the nineteenth-century criticism she is so right to consider suspect. That is, its tendency to primitivize and demean the Old Testament, encouraging the belief that it was full of ideas Western culture would be well rid of, that it revealed the "negativity and intolerance," in Assmann's words, of the Jewish mind. A favorite disparagement has always been that the Hebrew scriptures have little reli-

gious meaning and reflect no spiritual aspiration. Every book I
have looked at proceeds from these assumptions without comment, as if no reasonable person could take another view. It is
perhaps worth noting that the contemporary literary-critical
sensibility is rooted in a milieu not so unlike the one that produced nineteenth-century biblical criticism and which was surely
influenced by it—in, for example, Nietzsche and Heidegger.

One last book is worth noting because of its utter, credu-
lous reverence for this same nineteenth-century biblical his-
toricism. Gerd Lüdemann, in *The Unholy in Holy Scripture: The Dark
Side of the Bible* (1996), quotes the following "classic" description
of Israel from the writing of Wellhausen, one of the great figures of that school:

> Then and for centuries afterwards the prime expres-
> sion of the life of the nation was war. It is war that
> makes peoples; war was the function in which the co-
> hesion of the Israelite tribes was first confirmed, and
> as a national war it was a holy business. Yahweh was
> the battle-cry of this warlike confederacy, the shortest
> expression of what united them and separated them
> from others. Israel means "El (God) fights," and Yah-
> weh was the fighting El, from whom the nation took
> its name . . . The war camp, the cradle of the nation,
> was also the oldest sanctuary. Such was Israel and such
> was Yahweh.

One would expect a scholar so clear-eyed and disabused as
Lüdemann tells us he is to note here the probable contamination of historical objectivity by the nationalist excitements of
the period during which Wellhausen did his work. This warlike confederacy wanted to walk back to Egypt when they
learned that the Canaanites were tall and their city walls were
high. And if the name "Israel" does actually mean "God fights,"

then the etymology offered for it in the narrative of Jacob's wrestling with an angel (Genesis 32:24–30), "he who fights with God," is a profound reinterpretation of the relationship of God and his people, asserted within Scripture, which does not at all confirm Wellhausen's account.

In Lüdemann's reading, the Old Testament, and particularly Deuteronomy, is a theology of holy war. By this he means genocide, a word he employs frequently. He is aware the evidence is doubtful that such warfare was actually carried out, but he offers a proof that it is indeed likely to have been practiced by the Israelites. His reasoning on this crucial point is enough to make one weep for the scholarly enterprise. He has found a Moabite inscription which declares that at the hands of one King Mesha "Israel (!) perished utterly and forever." Having made his case to his satisfaction, Lüdemann goes on to aggrandize this genocidal bent he finds in Old Testament theology, which he is obliged to do because, at very worst, holy war would have been a minor phenomenon simply through lack of occasion. Lüdemann says:

> The Holy War, which in most cases was only longed for and not waged, and the message of Deuteronomy, are loaded with violence, and those responsible for them wanted in their minds to exterminate whole peoples in the name of God. The phenomena mentioned are only the shell outside a glowing kernel. Its content is the claim to exclusiveness made by an intolerant deity or, more precisely, the image of an intolerant God who chooses Israel and for better or for worse has sworn an oath with this people.

This is how the little wars and imagined wars of the Israelites become the very big and very real wars of the Europeans. The next stage in Lüdemann's argument is inevitable, there-

fore. "The most pernicious consequence of the utopias of violence in the Old Testament which are bound up with the Holy
War is that in the history of Christian influence, from the
Crusades to the Holocaust, they were turned against the people
in whose tradition they were produced." Once again we know
who to blame.

Lüdemann says, "anti-Judaism was and is the creeping poison in the history of Christianity. Whether it has already passed
its climax in the history of the Christian churches and theology
remains to be seen." No student of the subject would dispute
either point. He continues: "At the same time anti-Judaism has
tragic features, since much in it has in fact been taken over from
Israel and later was even [*sic*] turned against the Jews. Part of
the real problem seems to be how a people can suddenly claim
that it has been chosen and *vice versa* [whatever that means]. For
election often provokes hostility to the others who have not
been chosen." So the problem all lies with the Old Testament.
The source of anti-Judaism is Judaism. This is astonishing.
And here is how Christianity is to be saved. The Old Testament
is to be put aside, and those parts of the New Testament which
are contaminated by its violence and exclusivist influences are
to be put aside, until we are left with Jesus of Nazareth, a very
nice man.

Miles remarks that the accomplishment of the Hebrew Bible is
ethical monotheism. There being one God, whose central preoccupation is morality, the preeminence of ethicalism over all
other values is established. Yet there is no hint in his account of
God of anything that deserves to be called ethicalism. Nor
does he pause to consider the meaning of the moral regime
established by God among the Hebrews. None of these books
views morality otherwise than as prohibition, or prohibition as
other than regrettable, though no doubt we all recognize that

those who have internalized certain restraints, against killing and stealing, coveting and slandering, for example, are not only better but also happier for having done so.

Yet there is an odd kind of magical thinking at work in these responses to the Bible. The assumption seems to be that if the Mosaic codes do not anticipate contemporary preferences in uncanny detail, their claims on our attention amount to imposition or worse. No one could bring such expectations to texts so very ancient as these are, who did not assume that they exist outside history and are therefore good or bad intrinsically, without reference to the circumstances of the culture within which they took shape. This is really only the flip side of fundamentalism. The notion that the laws ought to be ahistorical is no more sophisticated than the insistence that they are in fact ahistorical.

These expectations, that the laws should have arrived ahead of us at whatever consensus prevails—among certain of us, at least—in this odd historical moment, make the shortcomings of the laws, thus defined, of exclusive interest. The whole character of the law is inferred from those aspects of it which seem most archaic and least congenial. Schwartz proceeds from gender relations to attitudes toward foreigners to patterns of property ownership, calling them all exclusivist. But foreigners (the Hebrews were "strangers" and "sojourners" in Egypt, so there is no doubt about the meaning of those words) were clearly meant to be treated with fairness and generosity. And ownership of the land was limited and conditional by any standard—a part of what it produced always belonged to the poor, for example. Bishop Spong dismisses the laws of the Torah on the grounds of tribalism, saying they only regulated conduct among Jews. This would imply that one may kill or steal from those one is forbidden to oppress.

If these laws belonged to any other ancient culture we would approach them very differently. We need not bother to reject the code of Hammurabi. Presumably it is because Moses is still felt to make some claim on us that this project of discrediting his law is persisted in with such energy. The unscholarly character of the project may derive from the supposed familiarity of the subject. Freud might say that, since the killing of the father is forbidden in any case, there is no need to fret much over the weapons employed. The law as resented tyranny is under assault and that is all that really matters. In other words, Moses is somehow our ancient contemporary, whose ancientness does not relativize his claims on us but instead only makes them more insufferable. Solon is dead, Lycurgus is gone, but old Moses is immortal, still menacing and accusing, warping our personal relationships and confounding our value systems. It really is interesting to discover how oppressed one can feel by laws with which one seems to have no meaningful acquaintance. If anyone could document that the obligation is deeply felt among us to forgive our debtors, then the case for the patriarchal dominance of Moses would be more persuasive. The fact is that the hardest of the laws, those comprehended in the phrase "open wide thy hand," are never even noticed to be resented.

If one were to argue that the attack on Moses is and always has been an attack on the very idea of ethical obligation, one could adduce by way of evidence, first, the fact that where Moses has been rejected, virtue has been of the kind Jesus described as tithing mint and cumin—a devoting of much attention to minor things. When the Bible was finally unleashed on Europe, it set off revolutions.

A second, graver point might be made, too. Every one of these books displaces ethical responsibility away from Christian or modern civilization and onto the Old Testament. Is it useful, is it even rational, to excuse oneself and one's own from ethical responsibility by any means at all, let alone by means that reinforce this worst prejudice? And in fact would not justice to Moses restore to this mysteriously religious society something urgently needed, a sense of the absolute biblical imperative of respectful generosity toward the poor and the stranger? When Jesus describes Judgment, the famous separation of the sheep from the goats, he does not mention religious affiliation or sexual orientation or family values. He says, "I was hungry, and ye fed me not" (Matthew 25:42). Whether he was a rabbi, a prophet, or the Second Person of the Trinity, the ethic he invokes comes straight from Moses.

Wondrous Love

I have reached the point in my life when I can see what has mattered, what has become a part of its substance—I might say a part of my substance. Some of these things are obvious, since they have been important to me in my career as a student and teacher. But some of them I could never have anticipated. The importance to me of elderly and old American hymns is certainly one example. They can move me so deeply that I have difficulty even speaking about them. The old ballad in the voice of Mary Magdalene, who "walked in the garden alone," imagines her "tarrying" there with the newly risen Jesus, in the light of a dawn which was certainly the most remarkable daybreak since God said, "Let there be light." The song acknowledges this with fine understatement: "The joy we share as we tarry there / None other has ever known." Who can imagine the joy she would have felt? And how lovely it is that the song tells us the joy of this encounter was Jesus's as well as Mary's. Epochal as the moment is, and inconceivable as Jesus's passage from death to life must be, they meet as friends and rejoice together as friends. This seems to me as good a gloss as any on the text that tells us God so loved the world, this world, our world. And for a long time, until just a decade ago, at most, I disliked this hymn, in part because to this day I have never heard it sung well. Maybe it can't be sung well. The lyrics are uneven, and the tune is bland and grossly sentimental. But I have come to a place in my life where the thought of people moved by the imagination of joyful companionship with Christ is so precious that every fault becomes a virtue. I wish I could hear again every faltering soprano who has ever raised this song to heaven. God bless them all.

There is another song I think about—"I Love to Tell the Story." The words that are striking to me are these: "I love to tell the story, for those who know it best / Seem hungering and thirsting to hear it like the rest." This is true. Of course those who know it best would be those who, over time, put themselves in the way of hearing it. Nevertheless, if Western history has proved one thing, it is that the narratives of the Bible are essentially inexhaustible. The Bible is terse, the Gospels are brief, and the result is that every moment and detail merits pondering and can always appear in a richer light. The Bible is about human beings, human families—in comparison with other ancient literatures the realism of the Bible is utterly remarkable—so we can bring our own feelings to bear in the reading of it. In fact, we cannot do otherwise, if we know the old, old story well enough to give it a life in our thoughts.

There is something about being human that makes us love and crave grand narratives. Greek and Roman boys memorized Homer. This was a large part of their education, just as memorizing the Koran is now for many boys in Islamic cultures. And this is one means by which important traditions are preserved and made in effect the major dialects of their civilizations. Narrative always implies cause and consequence. It creates paradigmatic structures around which experience can be ordered, and this certainly would account for the craving for it, which might as well be called a need. Homer was taken to have great moral significance, as the Koran surely does, so there is nothing random in the choices civilizations make when literatures are sacred to them. I have a theory that the churches fill on Christmas and Easter because it is on these days that the two most startling moments in the Christian narrative can be heard again. In these two moments, narrative fractures the continuities of history. It becomes so beautiful as to acquire a unique authority, a weight of meaning history cannot approach. The stories really will be told again on these days because a parsing of the text would diminish the richness that, to borrow a phrase from the old Puritan John Robinson, shines forth from the holy Word. And everyone knows the songs, especially at Christmas, and becomes in that hour another teller of the story embedded in them. What child is this? A very profound question. Christmas and Easter are so full of church pageant and family custom that it is entirely possible to forget how the stories told on these two days did indeed rupture history and leave the world changed, implausible as that may seem. At the same time, they have created a profound continuity. If we sometimes feel adrift from humankind, as if our technology-mediated life on this planet has deprived us of the brilliance of the night sky, the smell and companionship of mules and horses, the plain food and physical peril and weariness that made our great-grandparents' lives so much more like the life of Jesus than any we can imagine, then we can remind ourselves that these stories have stirred billions of souls over thousands of years, just as they stir our souls, and our children's. What gives them their power? They tell us that there is a great love that has intervened in history, making itself known in terms that are startlingly, and inexhaustibly, palpable to us as human beings. They are tales of love, lovingly enacted once, and afterward cherished and re-told—by the grace of God, certainly, because they are, after all, the narrative of an obscure life in a minor province. Caesar Augustus was also said to be divine, and there aren't any songs about him.

We here, we Christians, have accepted the stewardship of this remarkable narrative, though it must be said that our very earnest approach to this work has not always served it well.

There is a great old American hymn that sounds like astonishment itself, and I mention it here because even its title speaks more powerfully of the meaning of our narrative than whole shelves of books. It is called "Wondrous Love." "What wondrous love is this that caused the Lord of bliss / to bear the dreadful cross for my soul?" If we have entertained the questions we moderns must pose to ourselves about the plausibility of incarnation, if we have sometimes paused to consider the other ancient stories of miraculous birth, this is no great matter. But if we let these things distract us, we have lost the main point of the narrative, which is that God is of a kind to love the world extravagantly, wondrously, and the world is of a kind to be worth, which is not to say worthy of, this pained and rapturous love. This is the essence of the story that forever eludes telling. It lives in the world not as myth or history but as a saturating light, a light so brilliant that it hides its source, to borrow an image from another good old hymn.

If we understand this to be true, what response do we make? How do we act? How do we live? We respond by loving the world God loves, presumably. But there is something about human beings that too often makes our love for the world look very much like hatred for it. Jesus said, "Do not think that I have come to bring peace on earth: I have not come to bring peace, but a sword" (Matthew 10:34). He said a number of things: "Love your enemies and pray for those who persecute you" (Matthew 5:44), for example, and "Put your sword back in its place; for all who take the sword will perish by the sword" (Matthew 26:52). But for whatever reason—as a Calvinist I propose the reason might be our fallen state—human beings and Christians have found obedience to the commandment to love one another modified by the statement I quoted first, which does not have the form of a commandment, though it has been taken to have the force of one, and it has inspired the response "Send me, Lord," with far more passion and consistency than the commandment tradition says is the last Jesus gave us, that we love one another (John 15:17). As a consequence, Christians have too often loved their enemies to death. Those enemies being, in the majority of cases, other Christians. The Inquisition is the most notorious case in point, but it is by no means isolated. Then as always the rationale was that those people with a different heritage or a different conception of the faith are not *real* Christians. They should be denounced, converted, or eliminated—for the sake of Christianity. And, fortunately, Jesus has provided us with that sword. This is a narrative that has been a major force in Christian history—God gives us the means and the obligation to smite his enemies. And we know who they are, so the story goes.

Jesus spoke as a man, in a human voice. And a human voice has a music that gives words their meaning. In that old hymn I mentioned, as in the Gospel, Mary is awakened out of her loneliness by the sound of her own name spoken in a voice "so sweet the birds hush their singing." It is beautiful to think what the sound of one's own name would be, when the inflection of it would carry the meaning Mary heard in the unmistakable, familiar, and utterly unexpected voice of her friend and teacher. To propose analogies for the sound of it, a human name spoken in the world's new morning, would seem to trivialize it. I admire the tact of the lyric in making no attempt to evoke it, except obliquely, in the hush that falls over the birds. But it is nevertheless at the center of the meaning of this story that we *can* know something of the inflection of that voice. Christ's humanity is meant to speak to our humanity. We can in fact imagine that if someone we loved very deeply was restored to us, the joy in his or her voice would anticipate and share our joy. We can imagine how someone bringing us wonderful news might say our name tenderly to soften the shock of our delight. The mystery of Christ's humanity must make us wonder what of mortal memory he carried beyond the grave, and whether his pleasure at this encounter with Mary would have been shadowed and enriched by the fact that, not so long before, he had had no friend to watch with him even one hour. Scholars use the word "pericope"—where does a story begin and end? How much we would know about this dawn, this meeting of friends in a garden, if only we could hear his voice.

I tell my students, language is music. Written words are musical notation. The music of a piece of fiction establishes the way in which it is to be read, and, in the largest sense, what it means. It is essential to remember that characters have a music as well, a pitch and tempo, just as real people do. To make them believable, you must always be aware of what they would or would not say, where stresses would or would not fall. Those of us who claim to be Christian, Christ-like, generally assume we know what this word means, more or less—that we know the character of Christ. For Protestants, this understanding of him is mediated through the Bible. Our saints and doctors, however brilliant and heroic, are rarely looked to for wisdom or example. The figure of Christ is our authority. No distinction can be made between his character and his meaning. No distinction can be made between his character and the great narrative of his life and death. But the fact is that we differ on this crucial point, on how we are to *see* the figure of Christ.

This scene, the account of the first hours of the Resurrection, written two thousand years ago in a dialect of an ancient language, by whom and in what circumstances no one can really know, inevitably raises questions. How faithfully did the writer's Greek approach the Aramaic of the original story—assuming that Mary would have told the story in Aramaic, and that Jesus would have spoken to her in that language? And how faithful have all the generations of translation been since then to the writer's Greek? It must be said of the origins of this powerful text that the Lord made thick darkness its swaddling band.

We understand even the narrative of the origins of the

narrative very differently. There are interpreters who insist on finding simplicity in just those matters where complexity is both great and salient. It is my feeling that reverence for the text obliges a respectful interest in its origins, and respect too for all its origins seem to imply about the kind of interpretation the text permits, as well as the kind it seems to preclude. I would say, for example, that the work of the group called the Jesus Seminar proceeded on assumptions that grossly simplify these questions and, in effect, impugn the authenticity of the text, as many writers have done over the last few centuries. Some humility would be appropriate—there are those who earnestly believe that *To Kill a Mockingbird* was written by Truman Capote. The limits to what can be certainly known about such things are narrow at best. I suppose most Christians assume that the creation over time of the Gospels and the New Testament as a whole was an event of at least as great moment as the giving of the Law to Moses, or the moving of the Prophets to voice their oracles. The literal "how" of these events we cannot know, but we have the Law, and we have the poetry. If some intervening rabbinical hand strengthened or polished either of them, this may only have brought it closer to its true and original meaning. I am assuming here that Providence might be active in such matters.

To return again to what has been called "the sword of the Lord": that phrase is itself an interpretation, since nothing in Jesus's words suggests that the sword should properly be called his. The note in the always useful 1560 edition of the Geneva Bible says of the divisions among families and households that are the effect of this sword, "Which thing cometh not of the propertie of Christ, but proceedeth of the malice of men, who loveth not the light, but darkenes, and are offended with the word of salvation." This same phrase does appear in Judges, where the sword is wielded by Gideon. The book of Judges is a somber and impressively clear-eyed account of the crimes and catastrophes that beset primitive Israel. If Gideon avenges his brothers in his rout of the Midianites, in doing this he also acquires power so coveted by his son Abimelech that he kills his seventy brothers in order to make himself Gideon's successor. And the phrase appears in fierce old Jeremiah, where it occurs as a lament: "Ah, sword of the Lord! How long till you are quiet? Put yourself into your scabbard, rest and be still!" (Jeremiah 47:6). The sword seems to have been wielded in this case by Nebuchadnezzar, who was attacking the Philistines. So this context does not support the idea that here violence is undertaken in the cause of righteousness by persons with any positive interest in the God of Israel. The prophet sees this disaster, like any other, as a judgment of the Lord, not as an endorsement of those who are his instruments in exacting it.

When he spoke these words, Jesus might well have foreseen that in bringing a new understanding of a traditional faith he would divide families—the "sword" he speaks of is the setting of fathers against sons and mothers against daughters. This is both inevitable and regrettable. In the narrative as I understand it, his words would be heavy with sorrow.

I have spent time over this phrase because it has been important in the history of Christendom and because I think it is important yet, an opinion I had arrived at *before* I looked it up on the Internet. Even among those Christians who are not so wedded to what some call literalism that they refuse to consider context, there is still an old habit of conflict within the household of Christ, the family of Christ, that flies in the face of that last commandment. To reach this conclusion I must assume that those who disagree with my understanding of Christianity are Christians all the same, that we are members of one household. I confess that from time to time I find this difficult. This difficulty may be owed in part to the fact that I have reason to believe they would not extend this courtesy to me. So it is with these conflicts in which we are so tediously entrapped, these frictions and disputes that have brought discredit to the faith we claim, and that resemble much too closely our approach to other faiths, to our further discredit.

Christian piety seems often to take the form of a rigorous narrowing of definitions, with the *filioque*, or the disputed nature of the presence of Christ in the Eucharist, or the disputed character of the experience of a second birth, shaping the history of the church, and also of the world—and rarely for the better, as people are very ready to agree, except in those cases where the controversy is one that enlists their own particular passions. Paul deals with contentions of this kind in the letter to the Romans. He says, "As for the man who is weak in faith, welcome him, but not for disputes over opinions . . . Who are you to pass judgment on the servant of another? It is before his own master that he stands or falls. And he will be upheld, for the Master is able to make him stand." And he says, "The faith that you have, keep between yourself and God; happy is he who has no reason to judge himself for what he approves . . . But he who has doubts is condemned . . . because he does not act from faith; for whatever does not proceed from faith is sin" (Romans 14 *passim*). Paul is addressing differences about what can be eaten, not surprisingly, considering the importance of dietary laws to Jews and the presence in the Roman church of Gentiles who did not observe them. This is not a minor issue, anymore than it would be now in a situation where these two groups were attempting to achieve one religious identity. So we can apply Paul's counsel to our case, if we want to, since the differences among us are less extreme.

But this may not help. In *Civilization and Its Discontents*, Sigmund Freud observed that the groups most prone to sparring were those most similar to each other, the Spanish and the Portuguese, the English and the Scots. He says, "I gave this phenomenon the name of 'the narcissism of minor differences,' a name which does not do much to explain it. We can now see that it is a convenient and relatively harmless satisfaction of the inclination to aggression; by means of which cohesion between the members of the community is made easier." This may be all it amounts to. Faith properly so called may not be the issue after all. The diversity of our country permits every religious group to think of itself as a minority, and as crucially dependent on group loyalty, so this "narcissism" might be a particular temptation in our case.

Freud also said, "When once the Apostle Paul had posited universal love between men as the foundation of his Christian community, extreme intolerance on the part of Christendom towards those who remained outside it became the inevitable consequence." This is not the contradiction it appears to be, really, since he assumed the impulse toward aggression to be a powerful and universal human trait under all circumstances. Still, we have seen too much intolerance and too little love to satisfy even Freud's morose expectations. And things are getting worse.

A narrative has emerged lately, a narrative of decline. It is about the loss of our religious and cultural essence, and it is stimulating in its way, like a horror movie or a panic attack. There is nothing especially American about this story. Indeed, Oswald Spengler and many others have made extravagant use of it. For our purposes it begins with the assertion by certain excitable people that this is a Christian country. So it is, demographically. And since this is true both historically and at present, attitudes and institutions that are Christian in their origins are profoundly influential in our culture. But this is not good enough. This influence is both unconscious and unforced, and it is therefore invisible to those who think that the majority religious tradition in the country, by virtue of its being the majority tradition, ought to be asserted very forcefully as an intrinsic part of our national identity. These people see an onrush of secularism intent on driving religion to the margins, maybe over the edge, and for the sake of Christianity they want to enlist society itself in its defense. They want politicians to make statements of faith, and when merchants hang out their seasonal signs and banners they want them to say something much more specific than "Happy Holidays." They say that the Founders meant to establish freedom *of* religion, not freedom *from* religion. Well, in fact, the Founders meant to give us freedom from *established* religion, from *state-sponsored* religion. Whether they themselves were religious or not is a separate question. I assume they were. But the country in its early period was largely populated by religious people escaping religious oppression at the hands of state churches, whether French Huguenots, Scots Presbyterians, English Congregationalists, or English Catholics. Freedom *of* was freedom *from*—the coercions that did and do arise when there is no wall of separation between church and state. Historically the freedoms of speech, press, and assembly were deeply implicated in religious freedom, all of them being violently curtailed on religious grounds through most of Western history. Since my own religious heroes tended to die gruesomely under these regimes, I have no nostalgia for the world before secularism, nor would many of these "Christian nation" exponents, if they looked a little way into the history of their own traditions. I suppose these old stories are seldom told because there is a reluctance to stir the embers of past conflict. Fair enough, though by telling them we might remind ourselves to be grateful for the religious peace we have achieved and to be wary of these instigators of new conflict.

Relevant here is the fact that Christianity does seem to have receded, and dramatically, in just those countries where there are established churches. I say "does seem" because in my conversations with Europeans I have heard a wistfulness and regret for the loss of Christianity. The established churches have defaulted, and to the extent that they are monopolies, their failures have closed off access to Christian life and culture. This is a broad generalization, I know, but it is meant to counter a broader generalization, that Europe is no longer Christian.

There is another narrative at work here, which feeds into the narrative of decline. Americans, for no reason I know of, take Europe to be the wave of the future and dismiss the fact of our vigorous religious culture in light of the supposed fact of the collapse of religious belief in Europe. It would seem that Americans have internalized a great prejudice against Christianity, assuming that it could not withstand the scrutiny of what they take to be a more intellectually sophisticated culture. How much anti-intellectualism, how much resentment of Europe and its influence, can be traced back to this prejudice? And how is it consistent with the belief that the church is the body of Christ, a belief I share, to think it has no intrinsic life to be relied on, and must, for the sake of its survival, be fastened to a more vigorous body, that of the nation? As I have said, this is precisely the wrong conclusion to be drawn in light of the many examples of nationalized and officialized religion that persist in the modern world. In general, this posture, this preemptive assault on secularism with all it entails, strikes me as frightened and antagonistic. Neither of these are emotions becoming in Christians or in the least degree likely to inspire thinking or action of a kind that deserves to be called Christian.

What it does certainly resemble is nationalism, territorialism. I am the sort of Christian whose patriotism might be called into question by some on the grounds that I do not take the United States to be more beloved of God than France, let us say, or Russia, or Argentina, or Iran. I experience religious dread whenever I find myself thinking that I know the limits of God's grace, since I am utterly certain it exceeds any imagination a human being might have of it. God does, after all, so love the world. If belief in Christ is necessary to the attaining of everlasting life, then it behooves anyone who calls himself or herself a Christian, any institution that calls itself a church, to bring credit to the faith, at very least not to embarrass or disgrace it. Making God a tribal deity, our local Baal, is embarrassing and disgraceful. John Winthrop said we would be a city on a hill—I believe it was Peggy Noonan who added the word "shining," changing the meaning of Winthrop's words. And if Calvin's commentary is to be trusted—and by Winthrop it probably was—she changed the meaning of Christ's words, too. A city on a hill cannot be hid. The world will see what we make of ourselves. These self-induced panics do nothing to enhance the respect the world has for us or for religion or Christianity. And to the extent that we are associated with Christianity we run the risk of defacing it in the world's eyes. I know there are those who feel it is unpatriotic to care what the world thinks. But just as discredited institutions close the path to Christian faith for many good people, undignified, obscurantist, and xenophobic Christianity closes the path for many more. I have the impulse, though not quite the confidence, to say, Woe unto those by whom the offense comes. I personally would not be surprised to see the secular enter into heaven before them. I know I presume in speaking in such terms.

I differ from these self-declared patriots not only in the assumption that God loves the nations equally and that his grace is meant for all of them but also in my belief that the United States of America has done many things right. It is not especially decadent, as modern societies go, and the notion that it is, is both tendentious and uninformed. I think our democracy has in most cases served us well—this again by the standards that obtain among human societies, which is the only reasonable standard to bring to bear on it. I am so unpatriotic as to believe that most Americans are good people, committed to living good lives, and that the expansions of freedom that have been achieved by us and for us in the last few decades have been a very great moment in our history and in human history. I suspect the edge of fear, or the passion of fear, that can be heard more and more in the national conversation may have behind it a sense that these great societal changes are not a new birth of freedom but a slippery slope to perdition. There is a disturbing lack of confidence in democracy in the frightened resistance to the workings of democracy and its continuous evolution beyond the old constraints of traditional society and authoritarian government. It resembles nothing so much as the disturbing lack of faith in Christianity that puts the darkest interpretation on social change, religious diversity, foreign influence, the implications of science, and so much else besides. If Christianity expresses the nature and will of God, and if Christ will be with us even to the end of the age, why all this fear? If the United States is the greatest country on earth, why so little respect for its culture and people?

I was traveling from Iowa to New York with my son not long after September 11. We passed a great many of those tall highway signs that usually advertise hardware sales and dinner specials. Most of them then said, GOD BLESS AMERICA. Only one of them said GOD HAS BLESSED AMERICA. Yes, he has. He has blessed us with one another. We have had an extraordinary experience here together. I don't think anything is more emotionally stabilizing, more clarifying in every way, than gratitude, especially in dark times. And we have more reasons for gratitude than we could ever count, or even be aware of. But respectful attention to those around us would help us to take account of the human wealth that contributes so much to our lives. Then why not trust? Why not enjoy the country God has blessed, in all its turbulence and variety, rather than judge and condemn, as if by a standard of righteousness God himself does not see fit to apply? Of course we have seen bad times, and we will see more of them. I am such an unregenerate liberal as to feel that much of what we suffer and will suffer we could also alleviate or prevent. In my Bible, Jesus does *not* say, "I was hungry and you fed me, though not in such a way as to interfere with free-market principles." I am so unpatriotic as to attach great importance to the day-to-day practical well-being of my fellow citizens. Until there is evidence that ideology mattered to Jesus, it will be of no interest to me. And we know now, if we want to know, how free and how wise and how principled those markets were, to which—for the greater good, of course—we subordinated practical concerns apparently so close to the heart of Christ, the feeding and clothing, the tending to the sick and respecting the humanity of the imprisoned. These good works, if they were assisted by means of governments, would make us like the French, they say. Whatever that means. I doubt that this notion is based on any actual knowledge of the French, but if it is, it certainly encourages me in the opinion that the secular have an excellent hope of heaven.

What can we know about the voice of the old America that sang those songs? There have been a great many voices. My own tradition traces its history to Plymouth Rock. I know nothing about my own origins, at least nothing earlier than migration to Idaho and settlement there. I adopted myself into Congregationalism on the basis of affinity, as most of its present members have done. I mention Plymouth Rock only to make the point that we Congregationalists need not defer to anyone in the matter of our tenure on these shores. That ought to make us American, by one definition, at least. Yet we are largely responsible for what the self-declared traditionalists call the empty public square. For a long time we considered the cross an icon, so it was not displayed even in our churches. So far from keeping the Christ in Christmas, we forbade the observance of Christmas, aware as we were of its pagan origins and associations. On our greens there was neither cross nor crèche, for reasons of faith and piety. This might give comfort, if it is comfort they desire, to people who take the measure of the presence of religion in a place from the public display of religious symbols. We also influenced the character of the American university. On the model of the Academy of Geneva and other European universities, our earliest colleges required an education in the sciences and humanities, a command of secular learning, before a student was permitted to study divinity. So perhaps the great American decline began with us, early in the seventeenth century. Or perhaps this is a narrative of origins that needs to be told again, to help us make a better interpretation of our own civilization, where it came from, and what in it is traditional, at least, if not essential. And that in turn could lead us to a new discussion of what is of value and what is under threat.

But all this is very parochial in the grand scheme of things. The great narrative, to which we as Christians are called to be faithful, begins at the beginning of all things and ends at the end of all things, and within the arc of it civilizations blossom and flourish, wither and perish. This would seem a great extravagance, all the beautiful children of earth lying down in a final darkness. But no, there is that wondrous love to assure us that the world is more precious than we can possibly imagine. There is the human intimacy of the story—the astonishing, profoundly ordinary birth, the weariness of itinerancy, the beloved friends who disappoint bitterly and are still beloved, the humiliations of death—Jesus could know as well as anyone who has passed through life on this earth what it means to yearn for balm and healing. He could know what it would mean to hear a tender voice speaking of an ultimate home where sorrow ends and error is forgotten. Most wonderfully, he could be the voice that says to the weary of the world, "I will give you rest," and "In my Father's house there are many mansions." It is a story written down in various forms by writers whose purpose was first of all to render the sense of a man of surpassing holiness, whose passage through the world was understood, only after his death, to have revealed the way of God toward humankind. How remarkable. This is too great a narrative to be reduced to serving any parochial interest or to be overwritten by any lesser human tale. Reverence should forbid in particular its being subordinated to tribalism, resentment, or fear.

The Human Spirit and
the Good Society

All thinking about the good society, what is to be wished for in the way of life in community, necessarily depends on assumptions about human nature. All sorts of things have been assumed about human nature, and have been found persuasive or at least have been accepted as true over the course of history. We have had a long conversation in this country about class, race, ethnicity, and gender, how the moral, intellectual, and emotional qualities attributed to those in favored or disfavored categories create the circumstances of their lives, and, as they do so, reinforce an acceptance of the belief that these qualities are real, these characterizations are true. When there were no women in medical school or law school, or in higher education, it was easy to believe that they would not be able to endure their rigors. We in this country are fortunate to have a moderately constant loyalty to the idea of equality that has moved us to test the limits imposed by these cultural patterns, some of them very ancient, some of them once virtually universal and now still deeply entrenched in many parts of the world.

Of course we have not realized anything approaching this ideal. The meaning of it is much disputed—does it mean equality of opportunity or equality of outcome? Frankly, if we were to achieve either we might find that it resembled the other nearly enough to make the question moot. In any case, our failures, real and perceived, sometimes manifest as an anger with the project itself, and this distracts attention from the fact that we have made a very interesting experiment, full of implication, in putting aside traditional definitions and expectations and finding that when they are not supported culturally, which is to say artificially, they tend to fade away. We can learn from our own history that the nature of our species, and our nature as individuals, is an open question.

I do not draw any conclusions from the fact of our apparent malleability. Certainly it cannot imply perfectibility. Since we don't know what we are, and since we have a painful and ongoing history of undervaluing ourselves and exploiting one another, we are hardly in a position to attempt our own optimization. Still, how can we find our way toward a fuller knowledge of ourselves? I have a favorite scientific fact that I always share with my students: The human brain is the most complex object known to exist in the universe. By my lights, this makes the human mind and the human person the most interesting entity known to exist in the universe. I say this to my students because I feel their most common problem is also their deepest problem—a tendency to undervalue their own gifts and to find too little value in the human beings their fiction seeks to create and the reality it seeks to represent. By means direct and indirect this problem has been educated into them.

I have a habit of browsing relatively respectable journalism to get a sense of the climate of opinion on this great subject, human nature. On CNN.com I came across an article which affirmed that liberals and atheists have higher IQs than conservatives and the religious. It explained the difference in terms of the tendency of intelligent people to act in ways that are not conventional, in the article a near synonym for "natural." Liberal is defined for these purposes "in terms of concern for nonrelated people and support for private resources that help those people." According to the evolutionary psychologist Satoshi Kanazawa, author of the study, which was done at the

London School of Economics but with American data, "It's unnatural for humans to be concerned about total strangers."

These very confident statements about human nature always seem odd under scrutiny. If the study should not be taken to imply that conservatives are less religious than liberals, then it must be taken to imply that religious people are less inclined than others to feel concern for people to whom they are not related. I'm sure all of us can think of a thousand examples that argue against this conclusion. But then the article seems to have a special definition of religion. I quote: "Religion, the current theory goes, did not help people survive or reproduce necessarily, but goes along the lines of helping people to be paranoid, Kanazawa said. Assuming that, for example, a noise in the distance is a signal of a threat helped early humans prepare in case of danger. 'It helps life to be paranoid, and because humans are paranoid, they become more religious, and they see the hands of God everywhere,' Kanazawa said."

Without assigning any truth value to any of this, for example his comparison of these groups on the basis of intelligence, I found myself pondering the assumptions embedded in it. Since it is intelligence that distinguishes our species and inventiveness that has determined our history, by what standard should an unconventional act or attitude be called unnatural? How can human nature be held to another standard of naturalness than its own? Perhaps with our intelligence comes the capacity to know about and empathize with the problems of strangers, and this makes it natural for us to do so. On grounds of their intellectual and practical limitations, bears in Canada must be forgiven their apparent indifference to the fate of bears in China. Under other conditions—bigger brains, opposable thumbs, bipedalism—for all we know they might be model activists.

The article suggests that people of high intelligence actually intend to impress others through unnatural behavior, here philanthropy. This sweeps concern for strangers back into the great category of self-interested behavior, which would seem to make it natural after all, granting the assumptions of those who find self-interest at the origin of all behavior. It would be a simple fix to broaden the definition of "natural" to accommodate observed behavior, seeing that the means of doing so are so ready to hand. But supposedly this concern for strangers is liberal, and Kanazawa identifies as a "strong libertarian," so perhaps a little tincture of self-interest has colored his conclusions.

It is characteristic of these queries into human nature that everything exceptional about us and about the situation in the world we have created for ourselves is excluded from consideration. It is as if a realistic view of the hummingbird required the exclusion of small size and rapid metabolism, or as if bees could only be understood minus their hives and their interest in pollen. There is actually some reason to worry about this kind of throwaway scientism, however transparently flawed, because versions of it are everywhere and because, whatever else it is, it is almost always presented as learned hypothesis if not outright "information" about our kind, assumptions about human nature presented as if they were objective truth and a reasonable and necessary basis for understanding reality.

Another article, this time from *The New York Times Magazine*, describes current thinking on the nature and function of the human brain as follows:

> [E]volutionary psychology . . . tries to explain the features of the human mind in terms of natural selection. The starting premise of the field is that the brain has a vast evolutionary history, and that this history shapes human nature. We are not a blank slate but a byproduct of imperfect adaptations stuck with a mind that was designed to meet the needs of Pleistocene hunter-gatherers

on the African savanna. While the specifics of evolutionary psychology remain controversial—it's never easy proving theories about the distant past—its underlying assumptions are largely accepted by mainstream scientists. There is no longer much debate over whether evolution sculptured the fleshly machine inside our head. Instead, researchers have moved on to new questions like when and how this sculpturing happened and which of our mental traits are adaptations and which are accidents.

This line of reasoning clearly assumes much, and implies much more, when it sorts human mental life into only two categories—adaptations that suit us to life on the primordial savanna and "accidents." All sorts of creatures are suited to surviving in their environments—this should be obvious on its face. The world would be a very empty place if it were not in fact axiomatic. Our humanity consists in the fact that we do more than survive, that a great part of what we do confers no survival benefit in terms presumably salient from the Pleistocene point of view. This kind of thinking places everything remarkable about us in the category "accidental," at least until some primitive utility can be imagined for it. If we were to step back and look at ourselves without preconception, if we were to say, for example, that we are what we do, then the fact of our biological kinship with the other creatures, which so far as I know has never been disputed, would not overshadow the indisputable fact that we are radically unique.

Every great question is very old. In the sixteenth century good John Calvin rejected "the frigid dogma of Aristotle," using the human faculties that exist in excess of or apart from physical need to argue for the existence and immortality of the soul. He said,

[T]he powers of the soul are far from being limited to
functions subservient to the body. For what concern
has the body in measuring the heavens, counting the
number of the stars, computing their several magni-
tudes, and acquiring a knowledge of their respective
distances, of the celerity or tardiness of their courses,
and of the degrees of their various declinations? . . . The
manifold agility of the soul, which enables it to take a
survey of heaven and earth; to join past and present; to
retain the memory of things heard long ago; to conceive
of whatever it chooses by the help of the imagination; its
ingenuity also in the invention of such admirable arts,
are certain proofs of the divinity in man.

To say that these capacities in us are "imperfect adaptations," accidental to our nature rather than essential to it, is to
exclude them from the degree of reality enjoyed by adaptations
appropriate to what is imagined as life in the Pleistocene, the
period of the last great ice age. Of course it would be easy to
make the case that our imperfect adaptations create the environment in which we as a species have lived for a very long
time, and which have changed the terms of existence for all of
life. Notably, they have given us the means to survive lesser ice
ages and inclement weather generally. To put the matter another
way, to begin with the assertion that we are primates after all,
and on that basis to discount the vast differences between us
and other primates, and to conclude on *that* basis that we are,
when all is said and done, simply primates with a great many
epiphenomenal qualities is circular reasoning to say the least.
And it is always worth wondering what we really know about
our cousins, the apes. Whatever else may be said about them,
they also have traits that brought them through the Pleistocene. As does every creature that has been among us for ten or
twenty thousand years—traits that differ from species to spe-

cies as traits tend to do. And *Homo sapiens sapiens* is a species unto itself, which might be expected to discourage facile generalizations, even if we had secure accounts of the adaptations that brought us and our kindred through the Ice Age.

Other disciplines have adopted versions of humankind stripped to what is proposed as its essence, that is, minus its most distinctive characteristic, its complexity. In a recent column in *The New York Times*, David Brooks, with whom I almost never agree, traced the recent economic collapse to the fact that elaborate theoretical models were based on a stick-figure anthropology, the idea of "the perfectly rational, utility-maximizing autonomous individual." This may seem incredible, looking back, but in fact I have had conversations with people who were entirely persuaded of the rightness of this model, and who could not be bothered with a glance at the historical record or at current affairs, or with a moment of introspection. We were awash in wealth, or something that looked like wealth, and the secret of unleashing yet more of it was adherence to the notion that markets were in some sense free, and should be even freer so that this perfect rationality and maximization of utility could have its full, beneficent effect. Simply stand out of the way, and the best of all possible worlds will emerge on its own, more or less inevitably.

This best of all worlds might not have been to one's taste, since it seemed to move toward its fulfillment with a vigorous disregard for the fragility of the planet and the finitude of its resources, and since it was driven by a calculus of self-interest that was materialist in the strictest sense of the word. Child labor on one continent produced a plethora of cheap and disposable gadgets for another continent, which fouled and wearied the sea in their transit. No matter. There was a rationality in it all that made doubts about the value of it, objections to the destructiveness of it, sentimental and retrograde. And unenlightened. That invisible hand was shaping—who knows what, really. I can't regret the fact that we will likely never know. It seemed to have the Midas touch, the ability to monetize virtually anything. Unlike that legendary king, who learned to lament his gift, it could also discount the worth of whatever resisted definition in its frankly mercenary terms.

Not so long ago there was a theory abroad that college professors should be paid per head of student consumer they attracted to their classes. The curriculum was to have been designed on the same basis, adjusting pedagogical supply to undergraduate demand. No more small classes in specialist fields, unless some corporation saw fit to underwrite them. No more retaining the capacity to teach in areas that might not be popular but might nonetheless have importance that in any present moment was unforeseeable. Whenever I hear monotheism or religious difference singled out as the great cause of conflict among peoples, I wish some part of the population at some time in their lives had been required to read Herodotus and Thucydides. The *Commentaries on the Gallic War*, that old staple of high-school Latin, could shed a little light on this very contemporary canard, a supposed insight that burst on us suddenly not because we had reached a pinnacle of enlightenment that allowed its truth to be realized at last but because whole literatures of relevant context had been, for all purposes, forgotten. How peaceful was the polytheistic world, in fact? Why did the nations so furiously rage together? Well, since we thought we knew all we needed to know about human nature, there seemed no longer to be any point in consulting human history.

One might have thought that this proposed streamlining of the institution toward economic efficiency would at least have been self-consistent. This seems to be one thing economy would require. All consequences should be harmonious if not mutually reinforcing, presumably. But we all know what sort of thing will fill a college lecture hall. Charismatic professors and unconventional topics are an important element in the university experience, to be sure. Less-demanding classes sometimes make it possible for students to take on other classes whose material is especially daunting or whose demands are especially great. And lectures that everyone talks about are a powerful leaven in a community of learning. But none of these things yield the other presumed desideratum of the University of the Invisible Hand, that is, an efficient, economically competitive workforce. So if the university were rationalized to produce the best teacher-student ratio, putting aside other considerations, it would lose the ability to produce highly disciplined graduates with the knowledge bases that would make them effective participants in an evolving world economy—and the emphasis here should certainly fall on "world." But to point this out was only to reveal a dismal failure of comprehension. Market forces would take care of the details, even the largest ones, and reconcile them all the more elegantly if only they were left alone to do their work.

It was a simple faith.

And like other simple faiths, it seemed for some reason to predispose its believers to indignation. It produced an oddly collectivist mentality, since whatever inhibited the working out of its great single law could be thought of as reducing the prosperity and economic freedom of every one—the emphasis here on "one," since it imagined an oddly atomized collectivity. Why should taxpayers have to support someone who teaches classical Greek to thirty students a year? Why pay an enormous tuition so that someone can teach modern Chinese to forty students a year? These inefficiencies are in effect a tax on individual wealth that could otherwise go into the great stream of utility-maximizing autonomous individual self-interest.

And what about social arrangements that might reward uneconomic choices, that would tend to shield the hapless and the feckless from the consequences of their own errors and deficiencies? By virtue of the totalism of this model of reality, they are everybody's business, everybody's problem. The fact that some upstanding producer/consumer somewhere is permitting her own power of rational choice to be diminished because she acts on a sentimental loyalty to her ne'er-do-well cousin or her beleaguered fellow citizens becomes, in these terms, not only foolish but actually wrong. Simple faiths tend to be driven to distraction by anomalies, and to bring an especially acerbic moralism to bear on whatever their belief systems cannot account for. If *Homo sapiens sapiens* is also *Homo economicus*, why all these deviations from the norm? If self-interest disciplines choice, why is society at every scale shot through with arrangements that seem to inhibit or defeat self-interest? One possible explanation might be that these arrangements actually describe human nature, mingled thing that it is. For this reason they are surely more to be credited as information on the subject than is any abstract theory. But no. There is instead the urge, driven by righteousness and indignation, to conform reality to theory.

This tendency has become generalized beyond the self-declared objectivity of economics. Cultural patterns replicate by analogy much more readily than they extend themselves by logic. We live in a time in which certain rather startling words have crept into American political discourse—Fascist, Stalinist, Maoist. If they have any legitimate use in this context, it is perhaps to draw attention to the recurrence of this impulse to conform reality to theory, as these ideologies all did in their time. In each of these cases there were infuriating anomalies—called cancers, parasites, bacilli—and otherwise known as elitists, dissenters, subversives, foreigners, persons perceived as foreigners or as defectives or deviants or more generally as threats to or burdens on the body politic. History being the greatest ironist, those who use the words "cancer" and "elitist" with reference to their fellow citizens now also use the terms "Fascist" and "Maoist," having added them to the lexicon of disparagement the Fascists and Maoists put to such effective use in dividing and devastating their own societies.

The economic theory described by Brooks is often called "capitalism," and to point to its moral and aesthetic shortcomings is therefore viewed in some quarters as unpatriotic, though, as Brooks points out, this late permutation of American economic theory has done the country catastrophic harm. Capitalism is presented as quintessentially American, though this form of it is deeply, and for some intolerably, at odds with many of our institutions, for example our venerable postal system. Noah Webster's 1840 edition of *An American Dictionary of the English Language* does not include the word *capitalism*. It does define "capitalist" as follows: "A man who has a capital or stock in trade, usually denoting a man of large property, which is or may be employed in business." This definition implies nothing like an economic system, let alone an ideology. I realize that my drawing attention to this fact in certain quarters might set off a hectic search for Webster's birth certificate.

Nevertheless, it seems important to note, before we ransack four hundred years of cultural development in the name of making the country more purely itself, that neither the word nor the concept is discoverable among our founding documents. It is everywhere, under the name "political economy," in Britain at that time, as it had been for generations. But Britain was the great power from which we were attempting to differentiate ourselves. Webster's *American Dictionary* offers a very general definition: "Political economy comprehends all the measures by which the property and labor of citizens are directed in the best manner to the success of individual industry and enterprise, and to the public prosperity. Political economy is now considered a science." Again, there is no suggestion of system or ideology, and nothing that particularly associates this "science" with America. The 1840s Webster's *American Dictionary* does include a definition of "socialism": "A social state in which there is a community of property among all the citizens; a new term for Agrarianism." And it defines "communism" as a "community of property among all the citizens of a state: a state of things in which there are no individual or separate rights in property; a new French word, nearly synonymous with agrarianism, socialism and radicalism." So some version of the modern vocabulary was current in 1840, the absence of "capitalism" being more interesting for this fact.

I suspect we have never come up with a term to distinguish our economy from others, though it is unique in important ways and has served us remarkably well. In fact it was not a system but a patchwork of experimentation well into the twentieth century. There is a fine, old, quintessentially American word, "pragmatism," that should serve well enough to describe the nonideological way we went about our national life in the days of our expanding prosperity. It did not have its full modern sense in 1840—Webster defines "pragmatically" first as "In a meddling manner, impertinently," but also as "in a manner that displays the connections and causes of occurrences." This is the essence of it for our purposes, engagement with reality as we encounter it in the world of experience. A practical response to occurrences, mysterious as they are, demanding as they are of vigilant observation and whatever can be mustered in the way of objectivity. Once we were innovators. Once we were credited with ingenuity.

My point is that our civilization has recently chosen to identify itself with a wildly oversimple model of human nature and behavior and then is stymied or infuriated by evidence that the models don't fit. And the true believers in these models seem often to be hardened in their belief by this evidence, perhaps in part because of the powerfully annealing effects of rage and indignation. Sophisticated as we sometimes claim to be, we have by no means evolved beyond this tendency, are deeply mired in it at this very moment, and seem at a loss to think our way out of it.

Yet there are other ideas floating around in the general culture, or fragments of information that could be the basis for other kinds of thinking, if we gave them any part of the credence we extend so willingly to the most brutally reductionist of these theories and their ilk. An article appeared recently in the Science section of *The New York Times* that described the discovery of stone tools on the island of Crete. According to the article, the tools are "at least 130,000 years old, which is considered strong evidence for the earliest known seafaring in the Mediterranean and cause for rethinking the maritime capabilities of prehuman cultures." If the writer is making a precise use of the term, I would consider this discovery cause for rethinking the definition of the word "prehuman," and therefore the word "human," taking behavior rather than anatomy as the set of traits by which humanity should be distinguished. The article goes on to say that "the style of the hand axes suggested that they could be up to 700,000 years old," since they "resemble artifacts from the stone technology . . . which originated with prehuman populations in Africa." Again, I find it a little startling to find the words "culture" and "technology" associated with creatures excluded from the category "human." Excluded on the basis of their physical configuration and cranial capacities, of course, but apparently capable of acting effectively on complex intentions, and of sustaining within their populations a body of skills worthy of the name "technology." This should suggest that the ability to teach and learn and to sustain skills and knowledge over generations not only preceded but formed modern man. According to the *Times* article, this discovery on Crete appears to be evidence that these prehumans "had craft sturdier and more reliable than rafts" and "must have had the

cognitive ability to conceive and carry out repeated water cross-
ings over great distances in order to establish sustainable populations producing an abundance of stone artifacts." How many
generations of refinement and transmission of skills would be
required to produce these crafts, good enough and numerous
enough over time to make this migration and colonization possible? Presumably life spans were short, and this would have ac-
celerated the process of teaching and learning, since mastery
would have to have survived despite the early deaths of most ancient artisans and sailors. In other words, it seems reasonable to
assume that life among these hominids must have been quite in-
tensely cultural and collaborative.

I am still using a journalistic source, so perhaps I am too
easily impressed by talk of stone artifacts and the geological
strata that yield them. All the same, comparison with the other
articles I have looked at does draw attention to the fact that they
proceed entirely—I think it is fair to use the word "entirely"—by
inference. The ancient hominid who weathered the last ice age
figures decisively in scientific understanding of the human
brain—which is really to say of human nature. Yet the hominid
itself is essentially hypothetical, the creature of theory. In him
or her we can recognize Brooks's utility-maximizing autonomous individual, the very creature, in the guise of the modern
producer/consumer, that has haunted our economics depart-
ments for these last decades. The hominid could probably even
be called perfectly rational, as animals generally are when they
negotiate the conditions of their survival.

I wish to suggest that there is more than coincidence at
work here. Modern theories of human nature, which are essentially Darwinist and neo-Darwinist, pare us down to our instincts for asserting relative advantage in order to survive and
propagate. This dictum hangs on our essential primitivity as
they understand it—assuming that our remote ancestors would
have been describable in these terms, and that we, therefore,

are described in them also. But it seems worthwhile to remember that this is a modern theory projected onto the deep past. Then the past, seen through the lens of this theory, becomes the basis for interpreting the present. And the observed persistence of these archaic traits in modern humanity affirms the correctness of this characterization of our remote ancestors, which goes to prove that these archaic traits do in fact persist in us. The endless mutual reinforcement distracts attention from the fact that it is all hypothetical. We know precious little about those dwellers on the savannas of the Pleistocene, and, as Brooks points out, we clearly know precious little about ourselves.

By some standards, 170,000 years ago is the blink of an eye. But it does take us back to the Pleistocene. Those prehuman colonizers of Crete seem to have left tangible information about themselves, if the report is to be believed, and this sets them apart from hypothetical prehumans. They could navigate at great distances over open water. Perhaps they had considered the heavens and had found a practical use for a knowledge of the stars. We have half-smothered out the stars with our cocoon of artificial light, but the ancients seem to have watched them endlessly. To consider means, etymologically, to take account of the stars, for the purpose of making a decision. Etymologically, a disaster is a bad star. These words are from Latin, which came late into the world, but which expresses a prescientific confidence in the inter-involvement of the cosmos and humankind. This sort of thing is reckoned primitive, so why should it not be among our primal traits? Perhaps it is excluded because it looks too much like metaphysics.

I am extrapolating, too. I can't help but wonder what history lay behind all this prehuman skill and purpose. So far as there is a visible trajectory from primitivity to present time, it suggests that creative intelligence appeared early. The neo-Darwinists would say this is all just an effect of genes seeking to propagate themselves. Of course the same might be said of every feature of all gene-bearing life, while the great interest of life lies in the fantastic differences among its forms. This is an instance in which a theory that explains everything really does explain nothing. It is rather like saying that life is an expression of the tendency of complex molecules to form in the bellies of stars. However true this may be, there is clearly a great deal more to the story. After all, human intelligence is not just a compliment we pay ourselves. It is a phenomenon of great interest in its own right. If it is rooted as deeply in our origins as artifacts suggest, in effect preexisting us by many thousands of years, and if its artifacts suggest teaching and learning, culture and cooperation, then surely we should be less invested in the low estimate of our ancestors, therefore ourselves, on which modern anthropologies depend. We should drop the pretense that we know what we don't know, about our origins and about our present state. Specifically, we should cease and desist from reductionist, in effect invidious, characterizations of humankind.

I would like to propose a solution of sorts, ancient and authoritative but for all that very sporadically attended to. What if we were to say that human beings are created in the image of God? It will certainly be objected that we have no secure definitions of major terms. How much do we know about God, after all? How are we to understand this word "created"? In what sense can we be said to share or participate in the divine image, since the Abrahamic traditions are generally of one mind in forbidding the thought that the being of God is resolvable to an image of any kind?

But it is on just these grounds that this conception would rescue us from the problems that come with our tendency to create definitions of human nature that are small and closed. It would allow us to acknowledge the fact, manifest in culture and history, that we are both terrible and very wonderful. Since the movement of human history has been toward a knowledge and competence that our ancestors could not have imagined, an open definition like this one would protect us from the error of assuming that we know our limits, for good or for harm. Calvin understood our status as images of God to have reference to our brilliance. He said, truly and as one who must have known from his own experience, that we are brilliant even in our dreams. There is much that is miraculous in a human being, whether that word "miraculous" is used strictly or loosely. And to acknowledge this fact would enhance the joy of individual experience and enhance as well the respect with which we regard other people, those statistically almost-impossible fellow travelers on our profoundly unlikely planet. There is no strictly secular language that can translate religious awe, and the usual response to this fact among those who reject religion is that awe is misdirected, an effect of ignorance or superstition or the power of suggestion and association. Still, to say that the universe is extremely large, and that the forces that eventuate in star clusters and galaxies are very formidable indeed, seems deficient—qualitatively and aesthetically inadequate to its subject.

I have made a long and indirect approach to my subject—the human spirit and the good society. The subject was of interest to me in the first place because I have felt for a long time that our idea of what a human being is has grown oppressively small and dull. I am persuaded as well that we educate ourselves and one another to think in terms that are demeaning to us all. I mean "educate" in the widest sense. The culture is saturated with information about the expectations we have of ourselves and one another. What we are taught in classrooms is a very minor part of what we learn from ambient experience, which will teach us that learning itself is suspect, not an attempt at some meaningful vocabulary of reflection but instead an affectation, a kind of idleness or triviality that deserves the name "elitism," and that has no purpose except to assert a claim to superiority.

Here the word "Maoist," used so loosely these days, really does come to mind. I had a Chinese student once who wrote movingly about a colony of exiles to the frontier of Mongolia who were treated as enemies of the people because they were mathematicians, or because they played the cello. This was done in the name of democracy. I hardly need to mention to this audience that if such standards had been applied at the time of the American Revolution, our democracy would have deprived itself of that whole remarkable circle we call the Founding Fathers, and your own Mr. Jefferson would have been the first to suffer denunciation. The Constitution, to which appeal is made so often these days, could never have been written. We are profoundly indebted to the learnedness, in fact the intellectualism, of the Founders, and if we encouraged a real and rigorous intellectualism we might leave later generations more deeply indebted still. But the current of opinion is flowing in the opposite direction. We are in the process of disabling our most distinctive achievement—our educational system—in the name of making the country more like itself. Odd as the notion might sound, it is well within the range of possibility. To cite only one example, I have seen trinkets made from fragments of Ming vases that were systematically smashed by Mao's Red Guard. If we let our universities die back to corporate laboratories and trade schools, we'll have done something quieter and vastly more destructive.

The lowering of ourselves in our own estimation has been simultaneous with the rise of an egoism based on the assumption that it is only natural to be self-serving, and these two together have had a destructive effect on public life. To cite only one example: Historically the United States has educated far more people far more broadly and at far greater length than any other civilization in history, and yet the notion is pervasive and influential that we as Americans are hostile to learning. Our colleges and universities—the greatest in the world by any reckoning—have come to be seen as anomalies because the love of learning that built them by the thousands is no longer considered a national trait, indeed, is considered a thing alien to us, despite such formidable evidence to the contrary. I know from visiting all sorts of institutions everywhere in the country that even the smallest college is a virtual Chautauqua of conversation and performance that binds it, together with its community, into national culture and world culture. I know from teaching and traveling elsewhere in the world that the role of higher education in this country is very exceptional.

Yet all this is unacknowledged as we sink deeper and deeper into the habit of mutual condescension, tending always toward mutual impoverishment, insofar as we can still consider ideas and information an essential form of national wealth. Journalism is an especially important instance of this phenomenon. The churches are, in too many cases, another. Over and above specific instances, and behind them, is a drift toward cynicism and away from mutual respect and from willingness to take responsibility for our life as a community and a culture. I know it is impossible to say this without seeming to idealize a past that was dreadful in many respects. But the difference between the evils of the past and the ameliorizations of the present is the measure of the willingness of earlier generations to acknowledge and act on needed change. These reforms were made in the name of justice. Justice is reckoned on the basis of our obligations to one another. These obligations are different, lower or higher, depending on the worth we are willing to grant one another.

·

As I said earlier, in the great matter of human nature, we seem to be able to be persuaded of anything, about ourselves and about others, as groups and as individuals. Granting these astonishing brains we carry around with us, granting the miraculous intricacies of the nervous systems of everyone we pass on the street, we seem to find nothing that will securely anchor ourselves or our species in our estimation. The very idea of human exceptionalism is held up to scorn, as if our doings on this planet were not wildly exceptional, whatever else may be said about them.

Thomas Jefferson wrote, "We hold these truths to be self-evident, that all men are created equal, that they are endowed by their Creator with certain unalienable Rights, that among these are Life, Liberty and the pursuit of Happiness." This is the kind of thinking I would like to recommend. We don't know the nature of Jefferson's religious beliefs, or doubts, or disbeliefs. He seems to have been as original in this respect as in many others. But we do know he had recourse to the language and assumptions of Judeo-Christianity to articulate a vision of human nature. Each person is divinely created and given rights as a gift from God. And since these rights are given to him by God, he can never be deprived of them without defying divine intent. Jefferson has used Scripture to assert a particular form of human exceptionalism, one that anchors our nature, that is to say our dignity, in a reality outside the world of circumstance. It is no doubt true that he was using language that would have been familiar and authoritative in that time and place. And maybe political calculation led him to an assertion that was greater and richer than he could have made in the absence of calculation. But it seems fair to assume that if he could have articulated the idea as or more effectively in other terms, he would have done it.

What would a secular paraphrase of this sentence look like? In what nonreligious terms is human equality self-evident? As animals, some of us are smarter or stronger than others, as Jefferson was certainly in a position to know. What would be the nonreligious equivalent for the assertion that individual rights are sacrosanct in every case? Every civilization, including this one, has always been able to reason its way to ignoring or denying the most minimal claims to justice in any form that deserves the name. The temptation is always present and powerful because the rationalizations are always ready to hand. One group is congenitally inferior, another is alien or shiftless, or they are enemies of the people or of the state. Yet others are carriers of intellectual or spiritual contagion. Jefferson makes the human person sacred, once by creation and again by endowment, and thereby sets individual rights outside the reach of rationalization.

My point is that lacking the terms of religion, essential things cannot be said. Jefferson's words acknowledge an essential mystery in human nature and circumstance. He does this by evoking the old faith that God knows us in ways we cannot know ourselves, and that he values us in ways we cannot value ourselves or one another because our intuition of the sacred is so radically limited. It is not surprising that the leader of a revolution taking place on the edge of a little-known continent, a man clearly intent on helping to create a new order of things, would attempt an anthropology that could not preclude any good course history might take. Jefferson says that we are endowed with "certain" rights, and that life, liberty, and the pursuit of happiness are "among these." He does not claim to offer an exhaustive list. Indeed he draws attention to the possibility that other "unalienable" rights might be added to it. And he gives us that potent phrase "the pursuit of happiness." We are to seek our well-being as we define our well-being and determine for ourselves the means by which it might be achieved.

This epochal sentence is a profound acknowledgment of the fact that we don't know what we are. If Jefferson could see our world, he would surely feel confirmed in the intuition that led him to couch his anthropology in such open language. Granting the evils of our time, we must also grant the evils of his and the cultural constraints that so notoriously limited his vision. Yet, brilliantly, he factors this sense of historical and human limitation into a compressed, essential statement of human circumstance, making a strength and a principle of liberation of his and our radically imperfect understanding.

Who Was Oberlin?

I recently reread Ralph Waldo Emerson's "Divinity School Address." The speech, which he delivered at Harvard to candidates for the ministry in 1838, was urgently critical of the state of American religion. He said, "I believe, with numbers, of the universal decay and now almost death of faith in society. The soul is not preached. The Church seems to totter to its fall, almost all life extinct." This is not the view we tend to have of religion in America in the early nineteenth century. After all, it was just at this time that the Second Great Awakening, a period of extraordinary religious ferment, had taken hold in upstate New York and New England. The fear of decline, more precisely, the certainty that decline is a present reality with an almost irresistible momentum, seems to be a constant of civilized life. It is a fear abroad in our own time, among people who would certainly assume earlier Americans could have had no such anxieties.

Emerson's concern is with the state of preaching. He tells these young ministers, "Let me admonish you, first of all: to go alone; to refuse the good models, even those which are sacred in the imagination of men, and dare to love God without mediator or veil. Friends enough you shall find who will hold up to your emulation Wesleys and Oberlins, Saints and Prophets. Thank God for these good men, but say, 'I also am a man.' Imitation cannot go above its model. The imitator dooms himself to hopeless mediocrity." So we may conclude that in early-nineteenth-century Boston, at least, Johann Friedrich Oberlin was "sacred in the imagination of men." As evidence of his wider influence we have a college in Ohio, founded by New Yorkers, that was already five years old when Emerson spoke.

Then who was Oberlin, and how did he engross the moral imagination of an influential segment of American society? He was born in Strasbourg in 1740 and died in 1826. He was a Protestant pastor assigned to an impoverished region in Alsace. According to the eleventh edition of the *Encyclopaedia Britannica*, "he set himself to better the material equally with the spiritual condition of the inhabitants. He began by constructing roads through the valley and erecting bridges, inciting the peasantry to the enterprise by his personal example. He introduced an improved system of agriculture . . . He founded an itinerant library, originated infant schools, and established an ordinary school at each of the five villages in the parish." That is to say, Oberlin was a social activist, a community organizer. According to *Appleton's Cyclopaedia of American Biography* (1875), "The result of his 60 years' labor there was, that good roads, bridges and dwellings were constructed, fine schools and comfortable hospitals established, and the agricultural products of the district greatly improved and increased, while the moral condition of the inhabitants was equally advanced." If the old language about moral advancement seems jarring, where standards of living and of education are radically improved we would expect the same kind of change, though we would describe it in terms we find more acceptable—less alcoholism, fewer thefts, a decrease in the occurrence of violence within families. The example of Oberlin made the case that organized efforts at social betterment had social betterment as a consequence. There are now people in important numbers who find this idea not only doubtful but ominous. It is not difficult to imagine what accusations would be flung at Oberlin in the present climate, and for this reason the fact of his great stature, indeed that he was held in a degree of veneration that Emerson found oppressive, and that his example was the stuff of American sermons, suggests that we might well take another look at the question of what is American and what is not, taking that word, as people often do, to mean something rooted in the history and tradition of the United States from its beginnings.

I will say at the outset that the word "American" is a remarkably difficult one to define, as it should be. At our best we tend to assume that change is at the center of our national experience, that we are good at change and have greatly benefited from it. So attempts at self-definition that exclude what have been formative influences, or preclude new ones, need to be resisted where possible. Despite this, the word is very frequently used as if it described a homogeneous population and a history and culture that can be characterized readily in few and simple terms. This is typical of its use at both ends of the political spectrum.

As an instance of this very pronounced tendency, and as an illustration of certain of its consequences, I will talk a little about a book that was on the *New York Times* bestseller list, titled *The Family: The Secret Fundamentalism at the Heart of American Power* by Jeff Sharlet. The book is an exposé, a history, and in effect an anthropology of the phenomenon called C Street. In case anyone has not heard of it, C Street is the address, and for many purposes the name, of a house in Washington, D.C. It is one of a number of houses near the Capitol where, for decades, men active in the national government, including members of Congress, have lived as a kind of secretive religious fraternity, apparently devoted to the project of putting political power to the uses of an authoritarian or theocratic version of Christianity. C Street has been associated through some of its members with a spate of those shabby sexual escapades we have grown so accustomed to hearing about, and largely for this reason it has been the object of media attention. More seriously, if Sharlet is correct, members have used their positions in government and the access to foreign leaders they give them to conduct a foreign policy of their own in the service of their own secret objectives. These are certainly grounds for grave concern. And if C Street tactics for acquiring and exploiting power really are modeled on those of Hitler, Mao, and Pol Pot, then the whole phenomenon needs urgently to be brought under public and legal scrutiny. The importance of Sharlet's subject is not to be doubted, if his account is accurate in its basic outlines.

Sharlet's book is relevant to my subject, the uses to which we put the past, because he devotes a long chapter to the origins of fundamentalism in America, looking at the eighteenth-century philosopher-theologian Jonathan Edwards, then at Charles Grandison Finney, a nineteenth-century figure who is less well-known but perhaps no less significant than Edwards for his influence on American civilization. The point of the chapter is to trace the origins of the least-savory aspects of the movement called C Street to the country's early, formative period. Having rooted fundamentalism as he represents it in the very medium of American history, he can, for instance, find the Marshall Plan to have been too conciliatory toward Nazis out of fundamentalist sympathy for authoritarianism. No mention is made of the profound difficulty of bringing any war to an end, nor of the lessons the American government drew from the disasters that followed the highly punitive Treaty of Versailles. This is to say, in Sharlet's view, the descendants of Edwards and Finney leer at us even from those moments in history that might otherwise seem highly defensible at worst.

There is a kind of perverse nativism in the idea that in important ways we are all, in all our diversity, living out the consequences of the errors and excesses of two preachers, one of whom lived and died a British subject, that is, in Colonial

America, the other of whom spent much of his adult life in the great swamp of frontier Ohio. Be that as it may, the effect of this genealogical approach in Sharlet's book is to generalize through the whole of American culture the impulses that eventuate in this odd, secretive movement whose purpose seems to have been precisely to subvert the norms and constraints that are generally assumed to govern American public life, and to subvert the policy objectives and the institutions of the United States as they do so.

We talk about the past in two important ways. On what is conventionally called the conservative side, those attitudes and qualities that are at present revered, or are at least polemically useful, constitute the very slender whole of historical memory. This approach treats context as an impertinence and change as decline. It yields a robust sense of loyalty to certain national values—a loyalty which is inevitably lacking in those whose reading of history leads them to draw up a different set of national values. Its certitudes do not provide the basis for a complex or nuanced view of either the present or the past.

Then there is the toxic heritage approach, the perverse nativism exemplified in Sharlet's use of Edwards and Finney. This is most common on the side of the spectrum conventionally called liberal or progressive. It treats context as irrelevant and change as never more than superficial. I am generally sympathetic with progressive positions, sympathetic with, for example, Sharlet's alarm at the apparently theocratic and cult-like Family. And therefore I am frustrated by the determinism implicit in his treatment of American history, which is, as I have said, only typical of reformist writers on what we call the left. Determinism and reform are at odds with each other, I need hardly say. The notion that reform has relatively little meaning reduces it from serious purpose to virtuous sentiment. And the sense that anything, here aggressive fundamentalism, is inevitable in this society goes a long way toward giving that thing legitimacy and even authority, toward making it, to use a potent word, American.

Charles Finney was a great reformer. His two signature causes were the abolition of slavery and the enhancement of the status of women. It is an anachronism to call him a fundamentalist, but he would certainly have called himself a revivalist. His preaching fueled the passions and largely channeled the energies of the Second Great Awakening, a religious excitement that began in upstate New York in the early years of the nineteenth century and swept the Northeast, persisting for decades. When precisely it can be said to have begun and ended is a matter of dispute, but it had many important consequences. It influenced and in many instances even inspired the settlement of the Midwest, a region that became a bulwark against the spread of the slave economy. Strikingly and crucially, it scattered a number of fine little colleges along the frontier, among them Knox, Grinnell, Central, Carleton, and Oberlin, all of them centers of abolitionism, stations on the Underground Railroad. I cannot generalize as confidently about the education of women simply because I have not researched the question, though what I know anecdotally encourages me to suppose that schools of this kind were also integrated by gender. Knox had a college for women, and the role of Oberlin in advancing the education of women is well known. The abolition of slavery and the advancement of women's rights were strongly associated in the period before the Civil War, though after the war, regrettably for them both, they were often seen to be in competition with each other.

Finney, typical of the preachers of the Second Great Awakening in his ability to rouse enormous crowds to extremes of emotion, to weeping and fainting, was also an epitome of the best of the movement in his commitment to these two causes, and in his association of them, at Knox College and then at Oberlin, with higher education. He himself was educated first as a lawyer, then as a minister, though his Greek and Hebrew were never especially strong. After extraordinary successes as a preacher in the major cities of the Northeast, he came to Oberlin in 1835 to assume the professorship of theology. He was president of Oberlin from 1851 to 1866. A fine musician, he was careful to encourage the study of music for which Oberlin is still distinguished, though the divinity school has long since departed for Vanderbilt. Finney presents in an unusually vivid form an important problem of American history. We have no equivalent figure now, though during his lifetime there were many revivalists who were also educators, highly cultured men committed to radical social reform—reform for them meaning legal, political, and social liberation. It would be difficult indeed to reckon the debt we owe them, both as individuals and as a culture, and just as difficult to imagine what America might have become, or remained, without their efforts and their influence. Our debt to them would be far greater and our society far healthier if the causes to which they devoted their lives had taken better root. But the revivalist style of religion, the passions and enthusiasms that surround it, lost their association with education and reform at about the same time that the country as a whole turned against racial and gender equality—that is, in the long decades, the three full generations, between the end of Reconstruction and the emergence of the civil rights movement. Perhaps the only modern figure it would be meaningful to compare with Finney is another preacher and reformer, Martin Luther King, Jr.

The Second Great Awakening has been remembered in history for its excesses and eccentricities. Associated with it were millennialism, spiritualism, and experiments with plural marriage. In many respects, notably the proliferation of communal societies, this period resembled the 1960s. New denominations arose from it, some ephemeral, some still vigorous. And there were those mass meetings, and occasional scenes of mass hysteria, none of them issuing in violence or destruction, a fact which should be remembered, since excitements of this kind are rarely so benign. That its reformist energies have been eclipsed by these other enthusiasms in the view of history may be accounted for in part by the fact that the enthusiasms outlasted the reforms as features of public life. And at the same time they made reform itself a target of ridicule. The contempt of a writer such as H. L. Mencken for popular religion is simultaneous and identical with his contempt for women's rights and his melancholy belief in the futility of efforts to improve the status of black people.

We live in a moment in which old conflicts, much altered during their subterraneous years, have boiled up again. The struggle to own the past so that it can be made to serve contemporary interests has led to gross distortions. But it is true also that the experience of any generation is inevitably a warped lens through which to view the thought and the actions of any previous generation, especially when there is a lack of rigorous historical perspective to correct for these distortions. This second consideration may go some way toward explaining the fact that there are *not* two sides to what would otherwise be a great national controversy. The present configuration of American culture leads us to assume that the revivalist style of religion must always have been hostile to reform and to the kind of education we call liberal, to assume that it must always have been obscurantist, antifeminist, and presumptively racist. The association of a figure like Finney with a college like Oberlin seems an anomaly, even an embarrassment. And the character of earlier American religious culture is assumed to have been of a kind with what is now called, by everyone on all sides of these is-sues, conservative Christianity. It is granted the authority by some, the inevitability by others, that come with the notion that it is America's old-time religion.

This brings me back to the book I mentioned earlier, Sharlet's *The Family.* As I have said, I am inclined to believe that there has been an encroachment on American public life by certain inter-ests who identify themselves as religious, whether in good faith or because religion, which is traditionally respected in this coun-try, offers them an entrée, a presumption of virtuous intent. Granting the reality of this phenomenon, and granting its importance, how is it to be understood? Sharlet begins before the beginning, with the career of Jonathan Edwards, whom he misrepresents radically and tendentiously, as he seems to ac-knowledge in an endnote where he says, "There are many great biographies of Edwards, but my method of research for this account of his life was to rely primarily on original sources, which I tried to read through the filter of my own half-secular mind and as I imagine a Family man might, attuned to power relation-ships." Then he offers a long and respectable bibliography of works by and about Edwards, a list of books so extensive, in fact, that one can only conclude the filter he mentions was very fine indeed, permitting the passage onto his page of virtually nothing except Edwards's account of the death of a young woman named Abigail Hutchinson, in which Sharlet finds evidence of something like necrophilia. I quote: "Did Edwards lust for Abi-gail? . . . Did Abigail long for more than the pastoral care? . . . 'I am willing to live, and quite willing to die,' she told him, 'quite will-ing to be sick, and quite willing to be well.'" At her death, Sharlet writes, "He [Edwards] had finally made her a woman . . . She was, at last, beautiful in the eyes of God, and of Jonathan Edwards."

There is nothing in the text to justify this very lurid interpretation. Accounts of saintly death are common to many religious traditions, Christian and other. But imagining this text
as read through the eyes of someone "attuned to power relationships" gives such an odd tilt to the whole issue of power
relationships, a tilt so little germane to Sharlet's argument as a
whole, that I incline to think Sharlet's motive is a more conventional one, that is, to give an unsavory character to American religion and culture from its beginnings.

This is indeed so firmly established a convention that "motive" is no doubt too strong a word. It may not have occurred to
Sharlet to do otherwise. I mention all this precisely because it
is a recent and relevant instance of an old "liberal" or "progressive" tendency—both words in quotes—to give the past away,
to make meagerness and pathology seem to be our only heritage. The great problem with this view of things, aside from
the fact that it produces mis- or disinformation, is that the
past has great authority in any society, and especially in a society like this one, where essential formative values and experiences are embedded in a fairly compact historical narrative. It
is an aspect of human nature to believe that who we are collec-
tively is a reflex of where we have been historically. For this reason among others the past should be approached with care and
with respect for the importance of history, even those moments
in it that are worthy of admiration. Sharlet's no doubt extensive
reading of the greatest metaphysician ever to live on this continent, that is, Jonathan Edwards, may well have baffled his half-
secular mind. This effect would necessarily be compounded by
his assuming the supposed perspective of a Family man, whom
he clearly, and perhaps with justification, considers fairly dull-
witted. Still, his research should have brought him to Edwards's
sermon "Christian Charity," in which he insists in very straightforward language on an ethic of unstinting liberality, that is,
openhandedness toward one's fellows. It is a text that requires,

indeed permits, no interpretation. Then we would have a frag-
ment of the past that could serve us in the great and deeply ignorant debate about whether generosity on a societal scale is
un-American, Communist, or, even worse, French. As we have
seen, Sharlet's emphasis falls elsewhere.

Edwards was a leading figure in the First Great Awakening, and Finney was a leading figure in the Second Great Awakening. So the character given by Sharlet to Edwards and his
movement establishes the terms in which we are to understand
Finney and his. I must stress again that his account of Finney
is important not because it is exceptional but because it is
typical, well-nigh inevitable. As I say this, I must acknowledge
that, again in an endnote, Sharlet makes it clear that his interpretation of Finney as of Edwards differs from that of scholars
in the field. "Rather," he says, "I mean to simply single out the
strand of Finney's life that I believe is most relevant to the genealogy of American fundamentalism as it has appeared in
recent times." So again, he has placed a filter between the reader
and history, as only those in a position to be surprised by his as-
severations and therefore inclined to read his note would be
aware. In the text itself he criticizes these specialists because
"they take a typical Finney proclamation such as this—'Knowing
your duty, you have but one thing to do, PERFORM IT'—and
consider it in light of debates over Calvinism . . . But they give
little credence to the words Finney felt must be capitalized.
PERFORM IT." Sharlet takes these words to urge believers to
theatrical performance, "the subtle delights and terrors of spectacle that link Finney's revivals to those of our present mega-
church nation." It seems fair to Finney to note here that, in the
words of a contemporary account, "Prof. Finney relied greatly
on doctrinal preaching in his revivals, as opposed to animal excitement, and his sermons were plain, logical, and direct."

As it happens, duty is not really a thing that lends itself to
theatrics. But Sharlet knows what Finney and perhaps any other

speaker of English means when he or she says one must perform one's duty. He notes, in a single sentence, that Finney was
"an abolitionist, a temperance man." In fact, Finney not only
urged those he influenced into active opposition to slavery, but
he also used his own potent presence against it very forcefully,
not least in coming to Oberlin, which was then, as he said, in a
great swamp in a mud hole, to help create a little society organized around the equality of classes, races, and genders.

In doing so, he embraced unpopular, deeply controversial
positions. There was such a powerful stigma attached to abolitionism before the Civil War, and after it as well—what fanatics these people must have been to hate slavery so much they
wanted to put an end to the institution altogether!—that to
this day it is treated as at best a dubious project. Sharlet names
"instances of overlooked religious influence in American history," including "the religious roots of abolitionism, the divine
justification used to convert or kill Native Americans, the violent pietism of presidents," ending his list with Jimmy Carter's
support for El Salvador, "the most murderous regime in the
hemisphere." This is probably not a conscious instance of guilt
by association, merely a lapse into the polemical language that
has clung to abolitionism since its earliest adherents suggested
that enslaving people was a crime we should desist from.

There is an odd tendency in American historiography to
ignore context. The society during the 1830s, '40s, and '50s was
profoundly troubled by the issue of slavery, and therefore union,
as it would be until these questions were finally resolved as a
consequence of catastrophic war. In what must be called our
relatively peaceful moment, we have seen again and again the
phenomenon of highly emotional crowds, not felled by a sense
of their own sinfulness, though no doubt some of them should
be, but aroused by questions having to do with the basic and
legitimate nature of the society, the power of the central government over against the states, and the beliefs and intent of

the Founders and the writers of the Constitution. Exactly these questions inflamed popular consciousness and fueled public passions in the decades before the Civil War. The abolitionists could quote a Founder, Thomas Jefferson, to the effect that slavery was a terrifying offense against the justice of God. If their crowds were at all of the same mind, a sermon on divine justice, even without any specific mention of slavery, might well have aroused emotion. While the religious cast Finney and others like him brought to public life seems familiar to us, this very superficial likeness should not lead to the kind of facile blurring that allows him to be represented by Sharlet as, in effect, the father of American religious charlatanism. Finney was no fraud. The passions he stirred in others were of a kind to have been put to generous and honorable use. Which brings us again to Oberlin.

I will speak very briefly about the founding of Oberlin. Its history is so remarkable that some may be familiar with it. On the other hand, it may be typical of other old midwestern colleges in that neither the institution nor the wider public has any sense at all of why it is here, or what it has meant. In 1833, a group of young men who had been students of George Washington Gale, a Presbyterian minister in upstate New York, came by way of the Erie Canal to study at Lane Theological Seminary in Cincinnati. Harriet Beecher Stowe, whose father and husband both taught at Lane, described their arrival this way: "The Lane Theological Seminary was taken possession of as an anti-slavery fortification by a class of about twenty vigorous, radical young men, headed by that brilliant, eccentric genius, Theodore D. Weld; who came and stationed themselves there ostensibly as theological students under Dr. Beecher and Professor Stowe, *really* that they might make of the Seminary an anti-slavery fort." Cincinnati, across the Ohio River from Kentucky and the slave states, enjoyed the economic benefits of the slave economy while it struggled with the consequences of being a largely unwilling refuge or transit point for fugitives from slavery. The situation was volatile, often violent, so "the trustees of Lane Seminary . . . voted that students should not organize or be members of anti-slavery societies or hold lectures or speak on the subject. Whereupon the students left in a body, and many of the professors withdrew and united with others on the founding of an anti-slavery college at Oberlin." Theodore Dwight Weld "led the secession which resulted in the transfer of all the students but six to Oberlin." These students, known to history, insofar as they *are* known to history, as the Lane Rebels, stayed for a time in Cincinnati, teaching black people and helping fugitives, supported by the New York merchant brothers Arthur and Lewis Tappan, until the Tappans found and underwrote this college for them. The Tappan brothers funded antislavery causes patiently for decades, though they were mobbed and their warehouses were burned to the ground. Lewis Tappan appears in the movie *Amistad* as the wan and tremulous fanatic who whispers that he wants the Africans who seized the ship to be killed, in order to advance the cause of abolition. The film is accurate only in one particular—Lewis Tappan did indeed organize the Africans' defense. The inevitability of the association of abolitionism with sick and devious motives and with hypocrisy is very nearly absolute. What is the opposite of abolition? Tolerance for chattel slavery, for human bondage. Why should pathology be associated with the cause of human freedom rather than with slavery? Political and economic interests come into play, certainly. Abolitionism did indeed have its roots in religion as Sharlet says, and he seems to find this deeply compromising. But this is a null factor, since equally impassioned religion was also deployed against it. To find the stereotype of the abolitionist reiterated, with emphasis, in a contemporary film, and to find its validity assumed in a recent book, when the creators of both the book and the film suppose themselves to be progressive—this is explicable only in terms of the dreadful potency of cliché.

But here in Ohio there arose a college funded by fanatics, learning its theology from a charlatan, populated by young radicals and their faculty sympathizers, named for a community organizer who was also, for heaven's sake, a Frenchman. What account did this institution make of itself? To quote an old historian, "Oberlin . . . became the first institution in the country which extended the privileges of the higher education to both sexes of all races. It was a distinctly religious institution devoted to radical reforms of many kinds. Not only was the use of all intoxicating beverages discarded by faculty and students but the use of tobacco as well was discouraged." So in some respects Oberlin was radically decorous, committed to a standard of rectitude respectable society at that time did not even aspire to. And what became of all that incendiary zeal? It spilled out in every direction, exerting crucial influence on the developing culture of the Midwest, therefore on the history of the country as a whole. Students from Oberlin scattered over the countryside, preaching and evangelizing, since those were the modes in which persuasion was done at that time, in that culture. They preached abolition, and they evangelized towns and settlements, one by one, for days or weeks, not leaving until they had persuaded the people there of the need to put an end to slavery. They launched a ground campaign. They initiated a grassroots movement. The effort was endless, dangerous, and exhausting. Weld, by all accounts the greatest of them, took a beating that permanently compromised his health.

Slavery was an enormous global commerce. The European countries that engaged in it, and most of them did, only *began* in 1888 to move toward a ban on the exportation of Africans from Africa to the West Indies and South America. Britain ended legal slavery in the West Indies in 1837, but it came very near intervening in our Civil War to preserve slavery in the American South, since cotton was a major part of its industrial system. In other words, a timely end to the practice was by no means assured. Abolitionist urgency, sometimes verging on desperation, is understandable in light of the overwhelming difficulty of the task they had set themselves. These students along with others created resistance to the spread of slavery as a lawful institution into the free states. If it had become established in the Midwest, it is difficult to imagine how it would ever have been extirpated from the country as a whole.

And Oberlin had offspring. The town of Gilead, an imaginary town that figures in my last two novels, is modeled on Tabor, in the southwest corner of Iowa. Tabor was founded by a group from Oberlin, including their leader, Reverend John Todd. It was intended to serve, and did serve, as a fallback for John Brown and others during the conflict in Kansas. The reverend had hundreds of rifles in his cellar and a cannon in his barn. A more typical feature of the settlement was a little college, no longer in existence, which educated women as well as men. Some of these women traveled to distant countries, Korea, for example, to help establish women's education there. History has ebbed away from Tabor since then, but it would be difficult to estimate the impact of this one little settlement on American culture and world culture—influence that derived from Oberlin. Over the years I have noticed but have not collected the names of other colleges with the same maternity. Berea is one of them.

Why does it matter whether or not this past is remembered? I will put the question another way: What was lost when this past was forgotten? We know from subsequent history that the ideals of equality these reformers lived out were not an aberration, that they lay along the grain of American cultural development, that they expressed an understanding of the implications of the founding documents which has been affirmed through legislation and Supreme Court decisions and has come to be acknowledged, by most of us, as quintessentially American. What would this country be now if justice, as it was practiced at Oberlin 160 years ago, had released the talents and energies and the goodwill of the great majority who in fact remained excluded? The classic American writers, Emerson, Melville, and Whitman, read very differently when it is understood that their visions of equality were not simply patriotic self-delusion but were being acted upon, bravely, strenuously, and, in the event, too briefly along the frontier, a region that may have come to symbolize freedom and hope on far sounder grounds than survive in our crude modern mythologies.

Cosmology

Edgar Allan Poe began to matter to me in what might fairly be called my childhood, my early adolescence. I more than forgave him his febrile imagination. In fact I loved the dark gorgeousness of his mind, and the utter, quite palpable, almost hallucinatory loneliness of it. His elegance and learnedness were his defenses, ironic, conscious, and pure for that reason. I have always thought of him as a man waiting out the endless night of his life with a book in his hand, some quaint and curious volume of forgotten lore, noting the smell and feel of the leather binding, the pretty trace of gilding on the spine, almost too moved by the gratuitous humanity of the thing to open it and put himself in the power of whatever old music still lived in it. Runes and rhymes, labials and sibilants, trying the sound of them under his breath, while the long hours passed. I read everything I could find of his, at some point even the essay—or as he would have it, the poem—called *Eureka*.

In 1848 Poe wrote a cosmology. The most remarkable thing about it is that it anticipates in many respects the account of the origins of the universe we associate with modern physics. Poe said the universe was born out of the explosion of an infinitesimal point. He proceeded to this conclusion by means of intuition and his own kind of reasoning, which, like everything about him, is so elegant as to seem suspect. He deduced that the irregular distribution of matter, in the form of stars, was the work of gravity. In such a universe gravity would therefore cause the universe to fall in on itself, to contract again to an infinitesimal point which would again explode.

What the fate of the universe might be remains an open question in contemporary physics, of course, and theories about it like Poe's are entirely respectable now, with the difference that, being Poe, he was persuaded the universe is at present contracting toward its end. He saw in the rhythm of it all a great beating heart. In his hands this is a frightening image. Still, the theory is consistent with theories current now, that our universe may be only one in a series, in any case not a unique event. We know now about the accelerating expansion of the universe. Poe would have loved dark matter and dark energy, even though they come at the cost of his ultimate vision of the narrowing perimeters of reality, so often imagined in his greatest tales.

It is moving to imagine him, hagridden as he was by poverty and alcoholism, grief and loss, and a slightly lurid reputation, pondering the great void and finding his way to an account of it through aesthetic reason, poetry. It is as if he embodied the history of humankind in his glorious mind and his very mortal person. Eureka. I have found it. What moved Poe to attempt a cosmology, and what made him so confident that he had indeed achieved insight into a great truth? The human mind at its mystifying work, endlessly, sometimes brilliantly, fitting myth and reason to reality, testing them against reality, just for the pleasure of it. Poe was not unaided, culturally speaking. There was the venerable doctrine of creation ex nihilo, the understanding of the first verses of Genesis as describing the emergence of the cosmos out of nothing. What made the ancients consider the heavens in the matter of their origins, and why were their intuitions so hauntingly sound, including the belief that the universe had a beginning?

As I remember, Poe read this long prose poem of his to a

large and receptive audience in Richmond. A second reading was scheduled but foul weather intervened to prevent it. And 1849, the year after its publication, was the year of his death. So this uncanny document was relegated to the back pages of the largest anthologies, neglected until twentieth-century science came abreast of it, then still no more than a curiosity.

I want to pose another ancient question, one we seem to have put aside in the last few generations, for all the world as if we knew the answer to it. What are we, after all, we human beings? It has been usual for at least a century and a half to think of human beings as primates, as we surely are, who developed certain traits that eventuated in a capacity for complex social life—I suppress the impulse to say "mere primates," since I suspect the other members of our great order are undervalued by us in the course of our devaluing ourselves. It is useful to remember that at other times we have thought about our nature in other terms, as creatures in time, for example. Moses Maimonides said that because time is so precious, God gives it to us in atoms, in infinitesimal, indivisible moments. Yet the potency of time is irreducible. Within an instant, said Maimonides, everything can be won or lost. His observation about our existence in time is true, whether or not one endorses the theological terms in which it is expressed. Centuries on we know no more about time than he did, or less, since we are not so attentive to it. And yet, moment by moment, every one of us experiences along with the whole of the cosmos this great mystery of being, this great unfolding of ineluctable, irreversible time.

There is dignity in the thought that we are of one substance with being itself, and there is drama in the thought that ultimate things are at stake in these moments of perception and decision. But the cosmos considered in such terms went out of style a few generations ago. We know that tremors pass through the sun as if it were a giant gong, that the earth tilts, that our hearts beat. But the thought of participation in reality on this scale seems to have been dismissed together with metaphysics as meaningless. In their place we have the casting back of anthropological assumptions to describe our remotest origins, which, by implication, also describe our essential selves. We have accepted this too readily as a kind of realism. I am not the first to suggest that anthropology arose in Western thought in an inauspicious period, one characterized by colonialism and so-called racial science. But I seem to be more or less alone in my conviction that, in all its primitivity, this anthropology continues to color the ways in which we conceive of human nature. And because it retains the old authority asserted for "science" at the time it arose, it functions not as hypothesis or theoretical model but as dead certainty.

I will make a suggestion that may sound like theology, and that is certainly compatible with theology, but might be useful all the same. In this universe of wonders and astonishments, perhaps we should allow for the possibility that something remarkable occurred in the eons between the emergence of whatever life-form began the movement toward humanity and the realization of this tendency in humankind. I would propose that there intervened a capacity for morally significant behavior, a singular capacity to do harm. And good as well, of course, though one crucial form of goodness, the ability to refrain from harm even despite our best efforts, is a gift we seem to lack. Essentially, decisively, we are at odds with nature. The theories of human nature that have developed in the modern period attempt to fold us into great nature by making human complexity accidental or epiphenomenal and by seeing in our capacity to do harm the most natural thing about us. This model of reality does not describe our history or our prospects.

At present, evolution is taken to have been propelled, in us as in all of life, by something called genetic "selfishness," which its proponents always assure us does not mean selfishness in the ordinary sense of the word, but which, extrapolated and applied, means this more or less exactly: the selfishness hypothesis, whether in the old Darwinist form that saw the world as endless competition among organisms for survival or in the new Darwinist form—Victor J. Stenger, in *The New Atheism: Taking a Stand for Science and Reason*, says "it is not the organism that seeks to survive but the genetic information that is collected in what is termed a gene." This theory has the appeal of offering a one-word answer to the question of how the world works. That genetic information can be said to "seek" survival or anything else may seem surprising, though the language of motive recalls the Freudian id or the Nietzschean beast, the self within the self whose impulses are lacquered over by repression and good manners. The new Darwinists are anxious, as their predecessors often were, to avoid the impression that they are indifferent to the fine arts and the finer feelings. So the primitive has been bounded in a nutshell, put at a discreet remove from manifest behavior. Yet it is still to be counted as the king of infinite space because its "seeking" is still the basis of all life.

Maimonides's comments about time are typical of ancient, medieval, and Renaissance thought in that they make of every life a great drama. The old pagan gods of the Mediterranean and the Ancient Near East were fickle and violent, easy to offend and hard to placate, but they weren't dull. And the fact that people attempted interaction with them means they thought of themselves in relation to their own creators and the creators of the universe. The exclusion of a religious understanding of being has been simultaneous with a radical narrowing of the field of reality that we think of as pertaining to us. This seems on its face not to have been inevitable. We are right where we have always been, in time, in the cosmos, experiencing mind, which may well be an especially subtle and fluent quantum phenomenon. Our sense of what is at stake in any individual life has contracted as well, another consequence that seems less than inevitable. We have not escaped, nor have we in any sense diminished, the mystery of our existence. We have only rejected any language that would seem to acknowledge it.

At its origin, this "modern" view is not the dullest conclusion ever reached by human thought on the subject. I have already mentioned "selfishness," that is, instinctive commitment to the survival and flourishing of self and kin at any appropriate cost to others. At best and at worst human behavior does not square well with a formula that would make the individual's well-being his primary interest and motive. So "selfishness" was ascribed instead to the gene. By this means actual human self-awareness and behavior were placed at a far enough remove from their biological origins to be more or less irrelevant to the question of the credibility of this theory. The slack between motive and manifest behavior means that we are utterly deceived in the matter of our true nature and the meaning of our choices, and so is everyone else. Character, in the fictional sense and in every other sense, is depleted to nothing, more or less—all this in order to grant the possibility of acts that have the appearance of being disinterested or generous. A duller construction of personality is possible. There might sometime be a resurgence of behaviorism.

The embrace of essential beastliness, made scientific and respectable by a reading of Darwin that may or may not have done justice to his intentions, thrilled and enthralled Western thought in certain quarters and in fact still does enthrall persons and groups who experience life in society as a barely tolerable constraint on a kind of freedom they consider a birthright. This freedom appears to have most of the essential features of a war of each against all, whether a hot war that compels them to go armed to Starbucks or to church or a cold war that makes a virtue of craftiness and guile, the ability to loot and wreck the national economy without getting caught. H. L. Mencken, translator, interpreter, and passionate admirer of Friedrich Nietzsche, wrote that someone who acquires a million dollars by dishonest means is superior, in Nietzschean terms, to an honest man who has nothing. This might be no more than a thumbnail sketch of values that have shaped the history of the world. Still, it is a history that those who have neither an open nor a concealed readiness to do violence, who consider "predatory" a word with negative connotations, might have hoped we had put behind us. But the evolutionary anthropology on which all this is based ironically does not allow for meaningful change. It tells us that in our essence we are the brutes we always were, and, by extension, so is everyone with whom we have to deal, except for those almost begging to be shuffled out of the deck, genetically speaking. I am describing a worldview that takes itself to be conservative, and in many forms considers itself to be fiercely anti-Darwinist. I have never heard anyone speculate on the origins and function of irony, but I can say with confidence that it is only a little less pervasive in our universe than carbon.

This worldview was dressed up in the frock coat of culture, the corset of civilization, by Sigmund Freud. Though it left us with only the dreary problem of managing our neuroses, it still retained something of the Darwinist drama in his retelling, endowing us all with the suppressed memory of, and impulse toward, lurid violence, while thoughtfully excusing us from the possibility of acting on it. The givens of Freud's system are the conventional assumptions of evolutionary anthropology. He spun his famous tale about primordial patricide and cannibalism to tell us again that civilization arose as a constraint on our instinctive nature, not because our ancestors had any positive inclination toward coexistence and collaboration but because the terrible murdered father was internalized through all generations in the form of a clutch of rituals and taboos. Therefore civilization itself was the product of the suppression of forbidden impulses, which could be transformed and given expression through a process of sublimation, whence the whole of humankind's higher attainments. Freud's insistence that this cannibal murder did actually take place in what may be called historic—that is, *not* mythic—time may seem bizarre. It is, however, simply a special instance of a general and persisting assumption that we know what our remotest human ancestors would have been like and that they very much resemble those supposed primitives upon whom Western inquiry had fastened its monocled gaze before and during Freud's lifetime. The same may be said of the insistence that a hypothetical primitive abides in us, and that we know enough about him to use him as a basis for understanding our own character and experience and for understanding human nature generally.

All this came up recently in a writing class when I asked the students to describe their assumptions about human motivation. It became clear that a number of them took for granted that the substratum of all behavior was self-interest, this understood as gratification of certain of those same uncountenanced impulses Freud had in mind. Now, my students are excellent, large-spirited people, really exemplary. There is no reason to suppose that either reflection or experience would have led them to so dark a view of their kind. But this notion of human nature was taught to them as true and, good students that most of them are, they have accepted it as true. And it has had significant consequences for their fiction. Specifically, characters they understand to be outside the effective range of social formation tend to gratify uncountenanced impulses with a high degree of predictability. And, true to the Freudian paradigm, highly socialized, which is to say middle-class, characters tend to dwell in the moral twilight of essentially contentless decency, which they frequently depart from in search of a truer self.

At either end of this very short spectrum we find persons understood as having radically limited self-awareness, a minimum of meaningful inwardness, very little real ability to choose or appraise their actions. In other words, they have little true individuality—that is, character. From a fictional point of view, this is a problem. From a political point of view, it is a particularly unattractive example of class bias, poorly compensated by the fact that the bias cuts both ways. When I laid out my sense of the origins and nature of the problem, when I suggested that it was indeed a problem, there was a moment of thoughtful silence. Then one of them asked, "If you reject Freud, what else is there?" She was asking what other model could be found for interpreting human nature. If a well-educated woman a third my age has to ask the question, and none of her peers is able to propose an answer, then the authority of Freudianism is clearly undiminished. And if at this point it has the potency of common wisdom or of folklore more than of science, its influence on thinking is perhaps only greater for this fact.

I pause here to ponder what I consider one of the most remarkable aspects of human nature, its profound tractability. In fact, its intractable tractability. When the subject is our own nature and the nature of our kind, something we all experience continuously and immediately, it is clear that we can be persuaded of absolutely anything, at whatever cost in personal misery and general destruction. Education of every kind, whether random or intentional, can have the deepest consequences for any individual's sense of himself or herself. Our ancestors seem to have been persuaded that they were souls and spirits. Very much in their society reinforced this ancient belief. Was it based in intuition? Superstition? Wishful thinking? Or the simple tendency of people to allow their culture to form their beliefs? Now there are those who reject the very idea that there is such a thing as a soul or spirit. Is this denial based on their own experience? Is it a consequence of the rejection of the cultural narratives that make a religious understanding of the self available? Is it an acceptance of cultural tendencies that seem to them most intellectual or influential or least open to challenge, or seem to be shared among their peers? Who can know, finally? Why we think what we think is another imponderable. That the mind is susceptible to any number of influences is beyond doubt. Also beyond doubt is the significance for the individual of the contents, processes, and conclusions that characterize any mind.

To be fair, in the largest terms there are sound reasons for our inability to know essential things about ourselves, to know what we are. For one thing, we have no way of knowing the true nature of the reality in which we are immersed, of the substance of which we are composed. This is the question that lies behind many other questions, notably those pertaining to the existence of God. I have followed this lately fashionable debate with considerable interest, impressed by the difference between the grandeur of the subject and the generally low quality of the controversy on both sides. One benefit of an interest in the human capacity for self-befuddlement is the fact that from this perspective foolishness itself emerges as a stream of relevant data. Not very long ago geneticists spoke of "junk DNA," which has turned out to be no junk at all but instead another compounding of the complexity of the once-so-legible genome. I think students of the history of ideas feel their work requires a weeding out of junk ideation, as if the true life of thought existed in and was carried forward by whatever in retrospect seems sound and viable. At any present moment, before retrospect can make its exclusions, the cultural atmosphere is thick with junk ideation, which is, in that moment, indisputably influential, even dominant, and therefore not to be excluded from any meaningful understanding of what we are and how we proceed over time. It is the collective expression of the individual capacity for error, which is continuous with our gift for hypothesis and no doubt crucial to our ability to learn and to imagine. My analogy breaks down because while "junk" was clearly a misnomer when applied to DNA, humankind can burst out of the constraining efficiencies of nature and generate ideas that, however potent, are really, truly, and at very best worthless.

Except as data. The fact that we can stand apart from elegant nature in this way is very interesting and certainly germane to the problem of describing our own nature. And since the spirit of the times urges bipartisan consensus, I am happy in the belief that the atheist side in the great controversy about the nature of ultimate reality would endorse the general outline of my thesis, even if they and I differ about the particulars. They do indeed categorize most or all religion and the thought and belief that surround it as junk ideation. Why nature, with its stringent efficiencies, did not weed out a proneness to error so pernicious as they take religion to be and to have been, why nature in fact allowed it to flourish through the ages in a degree that made it virtually universal across human cultures is for them to solve. Their answer to questions about origins and persistence, when they touch on other features of animal life, is that they confer survival benefits, or at least are not incompatible with survival. Consistency would surely oblige a respectful agnosticism on the subject of the value to the species of religion, since it and its carriers do indeed survive and propagate. If these new atheists are, to their minds, taking the part of nature, ridding it of an anomaly it should have extinguished hundreds or thousands of generations ago, then they are not acting consistently with their stated fealty to the observable world, the world as it is. I differ from them in that I assume anomaly. That is to say, I assume that there are structures of meaning that do not align themselves with reason, insofar as reason operates within the closed system of neo-Darwinist reality. Earthly nature may be parsimonious, but the human mind is prodigal, itself an anomaly that in its wealth of error as well as of insight is exceptional, utterly unique as far as we know, properly an object of wonder.

Stenger responds to the question of the reason for religion this way. "[E]volution does produce evil, such as all the gratu-itous suffering in nature. So why shouldn't it be capable of producing the evil of religion?" But, Darwinistically speaking, can the suffering in nature be called gratuitous? "Gratuitous" is not a synonym for "regrettable." A general capacity for pain is essential to the survival of an organism, after all. Suffering that might be attributed to evolution is either a negative stim-ulus to self-preservation or a consequence of failure in the struggle to survive, whether the failure is individual or genetic. That is to say, suffering is a factor in the working out of evolu-tion, therefore not gratuitous. If religion is to be thought of as evil in the same sense, then it must also be granted its place in the natural order. If it differs from physical suffering in that it is extraneous to the natural order, then it is given an excep-tional status requiring a kind of explanation that would take the question of its origins and character outside the terms of evolution. The new atheists do not concede that there *are* other legitimate terms for the origins of anything. So religion as Stenger understands it is clearly a gross anomaly in the terms of his own system. And, scientifically speaking, fact should surely take precedent over any system in whose terms it is anomalous.

Religion is often represented as a primitive attempt to ex-plain phenomena which are properly within the purview of science. The neo-Darwinism urged on the world by the new and newer atheists claims to explain phenomena traditionally within the purview of religion—that is, it claims to explain absolutely and fundamentally everything. Not only the origin and nature of being but also its meaning, which would of course include the absence of meaning. When neo-Darwinism makes this claim it typically calls itself science, though science in any broader sense seems to content itself, very fruitfully, with the disciplines of hypothesis and inquiry.

In the middle of the nineteenth century Auguste Comte

asserted with utmost confidence that science, by then, he said, essentially complete, had discredited and supplanted religion. A few years later, perhaps in part because Comte had readied the way for this interpretation of it, Darwin's theory of evolution was also widely understood to have discredited and supplanted religion. So the "modern" image of science as the anti-theology was established before Abraham Lincoln took office. At that time the germ theory of disease was not established. The significance of Gregor Mendel's discovery of genetic inheritance was still to be recognized. Atoms were not yet known to have particles. Not long before, Poe had published his *Eureka* to general indifference. Yet already in that gaslit, horse-drawn era, at the tentative beginnings of modern science, certain grand implications, so familiar to us now, were trumpeted as inevitable, as they have been ever since. Whether so great a determination as this could be justified, the heavens declared empty, on the basis of then present knowledge, one may reasonably doubt. But, true to the spirit of his time, Comte's primary interest was in imagining a total transformation of society. The French Revolution had experimented with the overthrow of religion on these same grounds a generation or two earlier, no doubt preparing the way for Comte, no doubt expressing a readiness in certain quarters to find a lasting and persuasive rationale for rejecting religion. Some might call this a prophetic insight into the future implications of science, some might call it an early instance of the polemical use of the mystique and authority of science. In any case, science, to its great credit, has transformed itself continuously since Comte. And yet the claim he made for it, that it had already discredited and displaced religion, has been made continuously ever since, in tones of sorrow or exultation, the same venerable conclusion arrived at again and again despite the always changing body of evidence—in part demonstrated, in much larger part discredited—offered in support of it.

We may grant the possibility that Comte was right in

foreseeing theological consequences in an emerging understanding of the natural world, and that these consequences
were, if not inevitable, then at least earned, despite the fact
that they also appear to have been determined by other influences than science itself. Nevertheless there is an abiding
problem in this tradition of thought. To this day, the reasoning
of the anti-religionists has the conceptual scale of nineteenth-
century science. While the new atheists are ready to embrace
the hypothetical multiverse, the idea that being has presented
itself over and over again in infinite iterations of which our
universe is one, in general the cosmos does not interest them.
The multiverse hypothesis is attractive to them because it answers, potentially, the questions raised by the apparent fine-
tuning of this universe to suit it to supporting life. If there are
any number of universes, odds are that one of them will have
these properties. One of them will be of a kind to produce and
sustain creatures like us, so it is no coincidence that that one is
the very universe in which we find ourselves.

If a positivist test were brought to bear on this idea, the
multiverse, it would be discarded as meaningless because it can
never be falsified. But in fact the idea is interesting and relevant for just this reason. Given what we think we know about
the origins of the universe, there is nothing implausible in the
idea that like phenomena of creation might have occurred any
number of times. Biblical and traditional conceptions of God
have enough of grandeur in them to accommodate the theory
without difficulty, so there are no religious grounds for rejecting it. Its importance to the new atheist argument lies precisely
in the fact that, true or not, falsifiable or not, it amounts to a
statement of the fact that our experience of being is special and
parochial, no basis for grand extrapolations from the structure
of the carbon atom or the fortunate placement of our planet
relative to its star. An even grander extrapolation, of course, is
the one that proceeds from the observed importance of genes

in transacting the business of organic life on this odd little planet to the insistence that, QED, there is no God. The being, or reality, that expresses itself in everything we know and are able to know may well find an infinitude of other expressions, unlike the reality of our experience in ways we cannot begin to conceive. Fine. But what is being described here, inconceivable and unknowable as it may be, is nevertheless the reality of which we are a part. If we do not know the character of being itself—I have never seen anyone suggest that we do know it— then there is an inevitable superficiality in any claim to an exhaustive description of anything that participates in being. And the assertion of the existence, or the nonexistence, of God is the ultimate exhaustive description. The difference between theism and new atheist science is the difference between mystery and certainty. Certainty is a relic, an atavism, a husk we ought to have outgrown. Mystery is openness to possibility, even at the scale now implied by physics and cosmology. The primordial human tropism toward mystery may well have provided the impetus for all that we have learned.

Consider the strangely persistent materialism of new atheist science. Its great confidence seems to be based on a fundamental error. It takes whatever has been observed and described as having been explained. To describe the processes of ontogeny or mortality does not explain why we are born or why we die. Users of the Internet have downloaded instructions for making compost and instructions for making truck bombs. Both involve nitrogen. Their differences are vastly more important than their similarities, however. If their components and their assembly are described, and even if their effects are noted, they are still not explained. Explanation would necessarily involve an account of the intention behind their making. So perhaps the very idea of explanation is an error of anthropomorphism when it is applied to things that do not involve human intention. The belief that divine purpose lies behind nature of course invites anthropomorphism because of the presumed likeness between God and humankind, the idea that the making of the cosmos was intentional in a sense meaningful to us. This may be where the habit arose of looking for the reason behind existence and event. Still, there is intention to be explained, human motive, which takes me back to that ancient question, the nature of humankind: Why do the things we do seem to demand to be explained, and why do they so often seem to defeat every attempt at explanation?

Let us say that in the years after World War II certain scientists and technicians built nuclear-power complexes that continuously released radioactive waste through pipelines into the sea. Let us say that over the years the industry grew and generated a great deal of waste of all kinds, including the most profoundly toxic materials known, which these scientists and technicians considered it both cheap and reasonable to dump into the ocean from ships. Waste dumping might become a highly profitable industry in its own right. Some of it would be tucked under the polar ice cap, some left in the landfills of the third world. But the sea is so large and so undefended that it would always be the depository of choice.

This would be a strange thing for scientists, ever the friends of reason, to have done and to have persisted in since 1957. But the story is true, of course, the very open secret behind the nuclear industries of Britain and Europe. I have never heard anyone describe the probable long-term consequences of all this. But those tons of silt and ash, uranium and plutonium, and a great deal else besides would generate heat continuously over the next few millennia, so they and materials contaminated with them would rise to the surface of the sea, where they no doubt already have had an effect on that one one-hundredth of an inch of surface that generates most of the oxygen in Earth's atmosphere. The sea itself is so crucial to the generation of the atmosphere that it should surely have a place in any discussion of climate change. True, its level is expected to rise and it is expected to yield fiercer storms. But its crucial capacity for generating oxygen and the fact that changes in the atmosphere may indicate that this capacity is compromised—these things never come up. I find this an odd silence. Perhaps scientists are not good judges of the consequences of their own work, even when its likely consequences are global and irreversible. Perhaps they indulge the common impulse to point blame away from themselves. The demographics of which the new atheists are so proud indicate that the persons responsible in this matter are themselves atheists. This weakens their claims for the superior reasonableness of atheists, and also for their innocence of the grand destructiveness they always attribute to religion. Granted, their motives are no doubt very familiar ones, money and status. Most religious traditions call these motives delusional, but for neo-Darwinists they are the core of rational behavior, tempered, of course, by a quasi-altruistic care for one's offspring, one's genetic immortality, a consideration which in this case does seem to present a conceptual problem, given the long-term impact on the biosphere that can be anticipated from large-scale radioactive contamination. These same scientists have often been called upon to inspect the nuclear programs of less-prosperous nations, just to be sure they were not doing anything unwise.

My subject here is human nature, which I will define for these purposes as the difference between a world in which there is a human presence and one in which there are no creatures more like us than the apes. What would we not find in such a world? One thing that comes to mind is damage. I am a humanist, profoundly impressed with civilization. But the fact is that nature did not need to hear the word "Eureka," or, for that matter, even the word "nature." I think we can assume that it would have been content never to inquire into its own workings. The presence of human consciousness is a radical, qualitative change in the natural order. What are we, after all? Why are we such mysteries to ourselves? Why do we stand apart from nature, even to the extent of posing a mortal threat to its continued life? It is a commonplace that human beings have a moral sense, though it is not obvious what this means. As a feature of individuals or cultures, religion or reason, it is unreliable at best and highly vulnerable to inversion or perversion. W. B. Yeats wrote of the world in his time, "The best lack all conviction, and the worst / Are full of passionate intensity." As we nod in recognition, it is important to remember that Yeats's sympathies were with fascism. What is striking is not only the fact that there is a more or less universal prohibition against murder but also the fact that there is a continual social and individual impulse to find exceptions to it, whether open or concealed. The striking thing about our species is that we create around us a vast *need* for a moral sense, to which our best instincts are clearly by no means equal. People say this sort of thing to one another when they hope to recruit us all to a higher standard, or to what, by their ever-fallible lights, they take to be a higher standard. My point here is only that our circumstance is interesting. The biologically enlightened often fret over our tendency to place ourselves at the end of an evolutionary sequence, as if we were its culmination. This is another effort to fold us into nature, to deny an exceptionalism that seems always to be thought of in positive terms. Mary Beth Saffo says, "Casual consideration of the average talk show, or faculty meeting, or the stupendous folly of environmental abuse, makes it clear that even our vaunted intelligence, a key to our evolutionary success, has its limitations." But every one of these things is a *consequence* of our vaunted intelligence, that same junk ideation that cannot be excluded from any empirical definition of humankind.

I quote from Stenger's *The New Atheism* because it is a compendium of bestsellers, as he calls them, by like-minded thinkers— Christopher Hitchens, Sam Harris, Richard Dawkins, and others—and because I have his book at hand. In any case, the degree of consensus expressed among books in this genre is remarkably high. If this is not what one would expect to find in the work of independent thinkers addressing the largest of subjects, at least it makes it easy to be fair to their argument. One factor in this consensus is surely that its essential conclusions are very old, and that its assumptions are few and simple. Real science no longer supports the notion that genetic mutation is random, the genome presenting itself indifferently to be winnowed by the asperities of the world. But no hint of a deeper complexity appears in this literature. The need to popularize might be an excuse, if the argument were not itself dependent on an extreme simplicity, an algorithmic iteration of relative advantage in genes and their phenotypes. Those entities better suited to survive and propagate do indeed survive and propagate. Those less well suited do neither. In the case of humankind, these writers reserve to themselves the definition of "better suited," declining the opportunity to consult empirical data. This very simple model has been extended to the flourishing of particular ideas—though not religious ideas—and even to the formation of the cosmos.

The conclusion I have been moving toward can also be stated briefly. The flourishing of these ideas, of neo-Darwinism in general, would not be possible except in the absence of vigorous and critical study of the humanities. Its "proofs" are proof of nothing except the failure of education, in the schools and also in the churches. If I were inclined to use the metaphors of contagion they so often employ, I would say our immunity to nonsense has been killed out, the flora of historical and cultural knowledge that education should sustain in us, and this has opened opportunity for notions that could not otherwise take hold. But I prefer a loftier metaphor, better suited to its subject. The meteoric passage of humankind through cosmic history has left a brilliant trail. Call it history, call it culture. We came from somewhere and we are tending somewhere, and the spectacle is glorious and portentous. The study of our trajectory would yield insight into human nature, and into the nature of being itself.

Notes

OPEN THY HAND WIDE: MOSES AND THE ORIGINS OF AMERICAN LIBERALISM

59 "America is a young country": George Santayana, "The Genteel Tradition in American Philosophy," in *Documents in the History of American Philosophy: From Jonathan Edwards to John Dewey*, 405.

59 "Calvinism, taken in this sense": Ibid., 407.

60 "the country was new": Ibid., 405.

61 "the Old Testament that was placed": Adolf Harnack, *Marcion: The Gospel of the Alien God*, 136.

63 "The God of the Old Testament is pictured": Ibid.

66 "There were giants in the earth in those days": Calvin, *Commentary on Genesis*, 246.

67 "that the liberal advance themselves": Calvin, *Commentary on the Book of the Prophet Isaiah*, vol. I, 413.

67 "There are indeed many occurrences": Ibid., 414.

67 "In this passage, therefore": Ibid., 410.

76 "But yet howsoever the case stand": Calvin, *Sermons on Deuteronomy*, 586–87.

76 "[A]lthough a man cannot set downe": Ibid., 583.

77 "The Lord commands us": Calvin, *The Institutes of the Christian Religion*, vol. 3, vii.

THE FATE OF IDEAS: MOSES

97 "this supposedly divine code" and "our churches are filled": John Shelby Spong, *Why Christianity Must Change or Die: A Bishop Speaks to Believers in Exile* (San Francisco: HarperSanFrancisco, 1998), 153–54.

97 "This mythology of a divine source": Ibid., 151.

98   "When citizens of China": Ibid., 13.

99   "a human father who would": Ibid., 95.

99   "The Jewish God in the Hebrew": Ibid., 47.

100 "lived in a world where cultural barriers": Ibid., 124.

100 his familiar theory: Friedrich Nietzsche, *On the Genealogy of Morals*, trans. Douglas Smith (New York: Oxford University Press, 1996), 18–21.

101 "to be short, Moses' law": Thomas More, *Utopia and a Dialogue of Comfort Against Tribulation*, ed. Richard Marius (New York: Everyman's Library, 1994), 31.

102 "For look in what parts": Ibid., 26–27.

103 "Israel is laid waste": James B. Pritchard, ed., *Ancient Near Eastern Texts Relating to the Old Testament*, 3rd ed. (Princeton, N.J.: Princeton University Press, 1969), 378.

110 "The God of the Jews": David Hume, *Dialogues Concerning Natural Religion and The Natural History of Religion*, ed. J.C.A. Gaskin (New York: Oxford University Press, 1998), 191–92.

112 "Though the law codes": Jack Miles, *God: A Biography* (New York: Vintage Books, 1996), 207.

112 "The equation is creator": Ibid., 93.

112 Miles acknowledges this: Ibid., 421.

114 "Strikingly enough": Jan Assman, *Moses the Egyptian: The Memory of Egypt in Western Monotheism* (Cambridge, Mass.: Harvard University Press, 1997), 167.

115 "by limiting": Hume, *Dialogues Concerning Natural Religion*, 160.

116 "Western culture is laced": Regina M. Schwartz, *The Curse of Cain: The Violent Legacy of Monotheism* (Chicago: University of Chicago Press, 1997), 68.

118 Schwartz draws attention: Ibid., 125–28.

119 "Then and for centuries": Gerd Lüdemann, *The Unholy in Holy Scripture: The Dark Side of the Bible*, trans. John Bowden (Louisville, Ky.: Westminster John Knox Press, 1996), 43.

120 "The Holy War": Ibid., 73.

121 "anti-Judaism was and is": Ibid., 124.

WONDROUS LOVE

133 "I gave this phenomenon": Sigmund Freud, *Civilization and Its Discontents*, ed. and trans. James Strachey (New York: W. W. Norton and Co., 1961), 72, 73.

THE HUMAN SPIRIT AND THE GOOD SOCIETY

144   On CNN.com I came across: Elizabeth Landau, "Liberalism, Athe-
      ism, Male Sexual Exclusivity Linked to IQ," CNN.com, February 26,
      2010.

146   "[E]volutionary psychology": Jonah Lehrer, "Depression's Upside,"
      New York Times Magazine, February 25, 2010.

148   "[T]he powers of the soul": Calvin, *The Institutes of the Christian Religion*,
      I.5.v.

149   "the perfectly rational": David Brooks, "The Return of History," *New
      York Times*, March 25, 2010.

155   "at least 130,000 years old": John Noble Wilford, "On Crete, New
      Evidence of Very Ancient Mariners," *New York Times*, February 16,
      2010.

WHO WAS OBERLIN?

165   "I believe, with numbers": Ralph Waldo Emerson, "Divinity School
      Address," in *The Portable Emerson*, ed. Carl Bode in collaboration with
      Malcolm Cowley (New York: Penguin, 1981), 82.

165   "Let me admonish you": Ibid., 87.

167   I will talk a little about: Jeff Sharlet, *The Family: The Secret Fundamental-
      ism at the Heart of American Power* (New York: HarperCollins, 2008).

168   And if C Street tactics: Ibid., 30, 216–17.

172   The contempt of a writer such as H. L. Mencken: H. L. Mencken, *Fried-
      rich Nietzsche* (New Brunswick, N.J.: Transaction Publishers, 1993),
      originally published as *Philosophy of Friedrich Nietzsche* (Boston: Luce and
      Co., 1913).

173   "There are many great biographies": Sharlet, *The Family*, 400n2.

173   "Did Edwards lust for Abigail?": Ibid., 66–67. Sharlet is quoting from
      Jonathan Edwards, *A Treatise Concerning the Religious Affections*.

175   "Rather . . . I mean to simply": Ibid., 402n7.

175   "the subtle delights and terrors": Ibid., 81.

175   "Prof. Finney relied greatly": "Charles Grandison Finney," in *Apple-
      tons' Cyclopaedia of American Biography*, vol. 2, ed. James Grant Wilson and
      John Fiske (New York: Appleton, 1887), 462.

176   "an abolitionist, a temperance man": Sharlet, *The Family*, 81.

176   "instances of overlooked religious influence": Ibid., 366–67.

177   "The Lane Theological Seminary": Harriet Beecher Stowe, *The Lives
      and Deeds of Our Self-Made Men*, rev. and ed. Reverend Charles E. Stowe
      (Boston: Estes and Lauriat, 1889), 252.

178 "the trustees of Lane Seminary": Jesse Macy, *The Anti-Slavery Crusade: A Chronicle of the Gathering Storm* (New Haven, Conn.: Yale University Press, 1921), 74–75.

178 "led the secession": "Theodore Dwight Weld," in *The American Cyclopaedia*, vol. 16, ed. George Ripley and Charles A. Dana (New York: Appleton, 1876), 546.

179 "Oberlin . . . became the first institution": Macy, *The Anti-Slavery Crusade*, 51.

COSMOLOGY

187 "it is not the organism": Victor J. Stenger, *The New Atheism: Taking a Stand for Science and Reason* (Amherst, N.Y.: Prometheus Books, 2009), 31.

194 "[E]volution does produce evil": Ibid., 63.

200 "Casual consideration": Mary Beth Saffo, "Accidental Elegance: How Chance Authors the Universe," *The American Scholar*, June 22, 2005, 18.